The *Orlando Furioso*

The *Orlando Furioso*
& its Predecessor

By the Rev. E. W. Edwards
Rector of Bicknor with Hucking

Cambridge: at the University Press

1924

CAMBRIDGE UNIVERSITY PRESS
Cambridge, New York, Melbourne, Madrid, Cape Town,
Singapore, São Paulo, Delhi, Mexico City

Cambridge University Press
The Edinburgh Building, Cambridge CB2 8RU, UK

Published in the United States of America by Cambridge University Press, New York

www.cambridge.org
Information on this title: www.cambridge.org/9781107634954

First published 1924
First paperback edition 2013

A catalogue record for this publication is available from the British Library

ISBN 978-1-107-63495-4 Paperback

PREFACE

THE edition of the *Orlando Innamorato* of Francesco Foffano has been used for quotations from that poem, for the *Orlando Furioso* the edition of Pietro Papini, and for the *Satires* that of Giovanni Tambara. The translations of the *Orlando Furioso* are, with one casual exception, from the metrical translation by Stewart Rose. Those from the *Orlando Innamorato* and the *Satires* of Ariosto are original, no English translations being available.

I have to express my thanks to the Syndics for the honour that they have done me in consenting to publish my book, and to the Staff of the University Press for the care that they have shown in preparing it for publication.

E. W. EDWARDS

April 1924

C O N T E N T S

I. The Romantic Tradition

IN his *Antiquities of the House of Brunswick* Gibbon remarks that, "In a period of near three thousand years five great epic poets have arisen in the world, and it is a singular prerogative that two of the five should be claimed as their own by a short age and a petty state." It is to be presumed that most persons of common education would know that the state to which Gibbon alludes is Ferrara, and that the poets are Ariosto and Tasso, whose births were separated by no more than seventy years. Some would be aware that, in truth, Ferrara deserves a triple crown, having produced in Boiardo, a poet superior to Tasso in force and originality though of inferior harmony and sweetness; but few, save specialists, could boast more than a superficial knowledge of these authors and their works, or could quote so much as a single line from either the *Orlando Innamorato* or the *Orlando Furioso*. Several causes can be suggested for this neglect of the poetry, and in particular of the epics, of the Italian Renaissance. It may be that the dazzling brilliance of its art has served to obscure rather than to illuminate its literary glories. Mere ignorance of the Italian language may often have proved an obstacle; for it has been said that Italian is less studied in England to-day than at any time since the fourteenth century. Yet this ignorance has not prevented a fairly widespread acquaintance with Dante. Allusions to the Florentine poet abound

E O   1

in our current literature, while Ariosto is seldom,
and Boiardo scarcely ever mentioned. The works of
English scholars tell the same tale. Many important
books have been written on Dante, and their number
is constantly increasing at a rapid rate; but few
students have concerned themselves with either
Boiardo or Ariosto; and, where they have done so,
it has often been merely incidental to the treatment
of some wider theme. This almost exclusive devotion
to the earlier poet cannot claim the support of more
than a single century; and that it is due to causes
moral, ecclesiastical or political rather than aesthetic
is evidenced by the judgment of the great Italian
critic, Francesco de Sanctis, that, as an artist, Ariosto
is Dante's superior.

Some might wish to urge that it is the study of
Dante rather than the neglect of Boiardo and Ariosto
that requires explanation. The best of English epics
are not easy reading. The worst are monuments of
inflated commonplace and pseudo-classical fustian.
With such associations, it is no wonder that many
should fear to embark upon foreign epics of unusual
extent and complexity whose beauties may well prove
too delicate for the clumsy perceptions of a northerner,
and whose unwonted idiom will double the length
of every tedious line. Yet these fears, however ex-
cusable, are, in fact, baseless. So good a judge of
literature and amusement as Charles James Fox
described the *Orlando Furioso* as being (together with

the *Odyssey*) "far and away the most entertaining of epic poems." Every reader will at once admit that tediousness is the last charge that can be fairly brought against either the *Orlando Innamorato* or the *Orlando Furioso*; and will soon learn that he is making acquaintance with productions singularly characteristic of the Italian genius, and therefore without any true parallels in English literature.

They are usually spoken of as epics, but their title to the name is, at least, doubtful. They have little in common with the *Iliad* or its successors, and the resemblances that exist are superficial, while the difference of tone and spirit is profound.

Their real affinities are with romance, whether in verse or prose, and their origins are to be sought for in the two great cycles of tales and legends which grew up in mediaeval France around the names of Charlemagne and of Arthur; nor is either poem intelligible without some knowledge of these, and of their Italian offshoots. Both classes of romance are extensive and varied, but certain characteristic distinctions have been noted between them. The Paladins of Charlemagne, the heroes of the *chansons de geste*, are primarily crusaders. Their warfare is against the heathen, their dominant impulse religious zeal. The battle is more frequently the centre of interest than the duel. There are few women and none are conspicuous. Love is not absent but its importance is not stressed. Sentiment is rare and

sentimentality unknown. The general effect is serious
and has been supposed primitive. Little attempt is
made to lighten it by humour.

The atmosphere breathed by the Knights of the
Round Table is different. The religious motive has
fallen into the background, and they fight more often
on behalf of their lady-loves, or to gain their approval,
than to win a victory over the Pagans. The whole
lives of the best-known heroes, such as Lancelot or
Tristram, are ruled by one over-mastering passion,
and in consequence the part played by women is all-
important. Sentiment is freely admitted, and is often
of an extravagant character. The battle has given place
to the duel, and the army of the faithful to the lonely
knight-errant. The emotional tension is sometimes relieved by scenes conceived in a light and jesting vein.

This is what may be called the common and traditional account of the main distinctions between the
Carolingian and the Arthurian romances, but it is
possible that this account may have to submit to some
modification when the results of recent enquiries
have been fully evaluated. For the above view of the
nature of these romances has grown up in close connection with a specific theory of their origin and
their relation in time. It was supposed that the
romances (i.e. the *chansons de geste*) of the eleventh
and twelfth centuries "were only the last result of
poetic labours that had begun several centuries before;
that the French epic was entirely 'spontaneous' and

'popular' in its origin, born of the events and expressing the sentiments of those who took part in
them; that the legend of Charlemagne and his companions is essentially the work of their contemporaries, that Roland and the others were first com-
memorated during their lives or soon after their
deaths." The researches of M. Bédier into the
history and character of the French epics together
with the confirmation that they have received from
the more recent and specialised work of M. Boisson-
ade upon the *Song of Roland*, have thrown grave
doubt upon this theory which may fairly be suspected
of owing something to the passion for explaining
phenomena, historical and otherwise, by reference to
a super-individual consciousness that marks a certain
type of German scholarship. The very complicated
train of reasoning upon which the views of M. Bédier
and his disciples are founded cannot of course be
given here, but they seem to have proved that neither
the *Song of Roland* nor any of the other *chansons* are
either primitive or popular, that they have no basis
whatever in earlier popular lays and that their connection with the historical Charlemagne or any of
his contemporaries is of the slightest. On this theory
the *chansons de geste* were inspired not by any events
in the time of Charlemagne, but by the numerous,
long-continued, and important crusades which the
French chivalry undertook, during the eleventh and
twelfth centuries, in aid of the distressed Christian

kingdoms of Spain. They reflect the spirit and the social conditions of that epoch, and are largely indebted for names and incidents to contemporary or almost contemporary clergy who were anxious to attract attention to various routes of pilgrimage, and therefore connected these routes with the adventures of sundry more or less fictitious heroes. The *Song of Roland* itself is the work of one man of genius, probably a Norman or connected with Normandy, and is not of a very early date. It was composed about the year 1120 and owes little or nothing to tradition; for, in the words of M. Bédier, "a masterpiece begins and ends with its author." It thus appears that the *chansons de geste* were not separated by any considerable interval of time from the earlier of the Arthurian romances; indeed some of these, such as the romance of Tristram, show traces of more primitive conditions than any which existed at the time when the *Song of Roland* was composed. It would, no doubt, be quite absurd to imagine that all this justifies us in trying to explain away the differences that have been noted between the Carolingian and the Arthurian legends, but it does perhaps allow a suspicion that these differences have been somewhat over-accentuated out of regard for a false historical theory, and suggests the need for caution until such suspicions have been refuted or confirmed by a new and careful examination of the texts in the light of M. Bédier's discoveries.

Of more direct interest to the readers of the *Orlando Innamorato* and the *Orlando Furioso* is the subsequent fate of these romances, both Carolingian and Arthurian. Their popularity was not confined to their native land. They were rapidly diffused almost throughout Christendom, and at least as early as the twelfth century were being eagerly read in Italy. Those northern parts of Italy where the social conditions approximated most closely to feudalism, and the common speech to the languages of France, were the first to feel their charm. They spread beyond the Apennines, and when Tuscan established itself as the literary language of the peninsula it became possible to meet the demand for translations. This demand, however, did not affect both cycles of romance to an equal extent. From the first the *chansons de ges e* had enjoyed the more widespread popularity, for they appealed not only to the educated but also to the uneducated classes who, though of course unable to read, listened eagerly to recitations in their own tongue of the stories of the Paladins. Interest in the Knights of the Round Table, on the other hand, was confined, broadly speaking, to those who had some liking for feudalism and comprehension of its ideals, and, therefore, prevailed comparatively little in Tuscany and districts of similar social organisation; and nowhere extended much beyond the ranks of the nobility. As a natural consequence the demand for translations of the *chansons de geste* was

keener and more persistent, but it is not in the field
of translation that the most striking difference between the fortunes of the two types of romance is to
be found. Both were translated, but it might almost
be said that only the *chansons de geste* gave rise to
imitations which had even the most modest claim to
originality.

In course of time immense numbers of such imitations and compilations were produced. The stories
of the Paladins, and in particular the story of Orlando,
became universally known to the remotest bounds
of Italy. Yet all this literary activity long continued
artistically fruitless; and at the beginning of the
fifteenth century, it looked as if Italian romance was
destined to sink below the level of literature without
having to its credit a single work deserving of remem-
brance. From this fate it was rescued by two men,
Luigi Pulci, whose *Morgante Maggiore*, of which
three parts were composed by 1470, is still worth
reading, and Count Matteo Maria Boiardo, who, in
1486, began the publication of the *Orlando Innamorato*, one of the masterpieces of Italian poetry.
Boiardo was quite independent of Pulci, but he was
not independent of tradition. On the contrary he
owed much to it, and both cycles of romance being
almost equally familiar to the noble knights and
ladies of Ferrara for whom he wrote, both contributed features of the utmost value to his work.
But their contributions were not alike. A choice of

characters was imperative, and all, practically without
exception, were taken from the Carolingian tradition;
of which alone some preliminary knowledge is
essential for the understanding of the *Orlando
Innamorato*. This tradition affected Boiardo in two
ways. In the first place, it fixed, not quite definitely
but within tolerably narrow limits, the character-
istics and mutual relations that he could venture to
assign to the chief figures in his story; and in the
second place, it enabled him to take a large number
of facts for granted because they were already well-
known to everyone. It is this latter circumstance
which creates difficulties for the modern reader, and
which makes it desirable to give some anticipatory
account of the traditional basis upon which Boiardo
worked before entering into any consideration of his
poem. It was made up of material relating to Charlemagne, to his Paladins and to his Pagan opponents.
Charlemagne is the Emperor. France he rules
directly, but England and even Scotland are subordinate to him, their kings attend him as vassals
and he can call for their help in case of need. He is,
if not old, at any rate advanced in years. He can
still go out to battle, but his are not the most striking
feats of personal valour. He is a feudal lord, not a
primitive sovereign, and holds his court at Paris surrounded by his nobles. Strictly speaking there are,
in Boiardo's view at least, only three Paladins, Orlando,
Rinaldo and Ruggiero, but no serious confusion will

arise if we venture to apply the name indiscriminately
to all the chief heroes of the Carolingian epics, so
far as they reappear in the *Orlando Innamorato*. The
Paladins are more important than the Emperor himself. They are not merely barons but are members
of the imperial house, related to each other and to
Charlemagne; their descent being given with exactness, though not always with consistency, by traditional
sources, as is evident from the genealogical tables in
Professor Rajna's edition of the *Reali di Francia*.

Foremost among the Paladins is Orlando. His
death at Roncesvalles, as related in the *Song of
Roland*, was really the nucleus around which the
whole cycle of Carolingian legends grew. Legends,
it must be remembered, which were to the contemporaries of Boiardo not entirely fabulous, but
which were supposed, even by educated persons, to
contain a considerable amount of historic truth; so
that it was possible to maintain, more or less seriously,
that existing noble families of Ferrara, as, for
example, the Estense themselves, were descended
from one or other of the Paladins.

To return to Orlando. He was the son of Milone
of Agrante and Bertha, a sister of the Emperor.
After a youth passed in comparative obscurity, of
which we are told in the *Aspromonte* and the *Or-
landino*, he was acknowledged by Charlemagne and
gave proofs of his strength and valour by winning
the helmet of Almonte, and slaying in battle Troiano,

the father of Agramante, the African King, whose invasion of France is, in one sense, the main theme of both the *Orlando Innamorato* and the *Furioso*. The helmet of Almonte was one of those marvellous pieces of armour, beloved of romancers, which men were ready to go any lengths to win, though it was, as Ariosto notices, of little practical value to Orlando, whose body was enchanted so that he could be wounded nowhere save on the soles of his feet. He was also fated to gain the victory over any opponent, however powerful, after three days fight. To us, all this seems rather childish, and neither Boiardo nor Ariosto were by any means blind to the ridiculous element in these tales, but they were not originally told in mockery, and popular feeling still regarded Orlando as a hero, and looked on him, and his feats of strength, with genuine admiration; a feeling which is echoed by Ariosto, though Boiardo has little of it.

Second only to Orlando in fame and favour was Rinaldo. Many readers will probably be aware of the fact that Isabella d'Este carried on a long and animated, though of course only half serious, controversy with Galeazzo di San Severino on the excellences of Orlando and Rinaldo; Isabella maintaining that Rinaldo was far the superior and Galeazzo as warmly advocating the claims of Orlando. Rinaldo's original is to be found in Renaud de Montauban, the titular hero of a very popular French romance, also called *Les Quatres Fils d'Aymon*, which was composed about the beginning of the thirteenth century. There were several Italian versions of his story, belonging to a later date, and neither Boiardo nor Ariosto need have been directly indebted to the French original, though very possibly they were acquainted with it. It may, however, be taken as representing with sufficient accuracy the popular knowledge of Rinaldo at the time when the *Orlando Innamorato* was being written. Renaud and his three younger brothers are brought to court by their father Aymon and presented to the Emperor Charlemagne. Renaud plays at chess with Bertolai, Charlemagne's nephew, and a scion of the house of Maganza. Through Bertolai's fault they quarrel, and Renaud, having appealed in vain to the Emperor for redress, strikes Bertolai dead with the chess-board. Charlemagne has not forgotten that Beuve d'Agrismonte, Renaud's uncle, had killed a son of his some years before, and though reconciled to Beuve, is implacable to this second offence. Renaud and his brothers are forced to fly, and take refuge in the Ardennes, their native district. We have here, perhaps, one of the reasons for the connection of Rinaldo and others with the Ardennes in the poems of Boiardo and Ariosto. They are exposed to great danger, for even their father is against them out of loyalty to the Emperor, but they are nevertheless able to maintain themselves until treachery delivers their stronghold into the hands of their enemies.

After seizing and hanging the traitor, they make their escape, but no other refuge is available for them in the Ardennes; and despairing of safety anywhere within the dominions of Charlemagne, they take service with the King of Gascony and build themselves a castle, the famous Montauban or "Hill of the Foreigner," from which is derived the title of Rinaldo di Montalbano usually given to Renaud in the Italian versions of his story. They do not, however, find themselves thereby secured from the vengeance of Charlemagne, who presently lays siege to Montauban with a vast army. Renaud has little help from the King of Gascony, who, at a later period, is induced to betray him into the hands of the Emperor, but he is no contemptible antagonist for, in addition to his own matchless strength and courage and the valour and devotion of his brothers, he has the aid of his cousin, Maugis. Maugis is not exceptionally distinguished as a warrior, but he is a great enchanter who commands the services of many demons. By means of his devices Charlemagne is entrapped and finds himself Renaud's helpless prisoner. Renaud, however, is too loyal at heart to take advantage of the situation and ultimately sets the Emperor at liberty without attempting to make terms. Maugis appealed to the taste of the age, and plays a fairly conspicuous part both in the *Orlando Innamorato* and in the *Furioso*, under the name of Malagise or Malagigi. Scarcely less valuable to

Renaud than Maugis, is his wonderful horse Bayard, who is not only incomparable in strength, swiftness and courage but is dowered with a human intelligence and a more than human loyalty to his master. He too reappears in our poems. In the original romance Renaud finally makes his peace with Charlemagne, and it is to this later period of his life that the *Orlando Innamorato* and the *Furioso* must be supposed to refer, for in them he figures as the loyal and devoted servant of the Emperor. Nevertheless the atmosphere of dignity and almost of reverence that surrounded Orlando was lacking to him, and he has not entirely forgotten his days as a robber-knight which his enemies also show that they can recollect well enough on occasion. In the popular fancy he is still the essentially good-hearted law-breaker and rebel, who is all the better liked for his independent spirit.

Renaud's brothers are of much less importance than himself, but his rescue of Richard, the youngest of them, from the gallows is obviously one prototype of the rescue of the same brother from death by fire which is attributed to Ruggiero in the *Orlando Furioso*.

Of the other members of Rinaldo's family, only his sister Bradamante requires notice. She also is a traditional character, but a much less conspicuous one than her brother. She figures in one or two minor Italian romances, and has there the warlike propensities and aptitudes which she displays in the works of Boiardo and Ariosto; but in the main it can be said that her character and her adventures as depicted in the *Orlando Innamorato* and *Furioso* explain themselves, and need little or no comment from outside sources.

Much the same applies to her lover Ruggiero. He was not unknown to tradition, and the fortunes of his mother, Galicella, are related in one of the versions of the *Aspromonte*. Boiardo and Ariosto, however, do not assume this tradition but take occasion to tell us as much of his ancestry and the events of his childhood and youth as their stories require. His treacherous death at the hands of the Maganzese was traditional, but falls outside the range of both authors, for Boiardo was prevented by death from bringing his poem down to this point, and Ariosto abandoned the idea, which he seems at one time to have entertained, of fulfilling his predecessor's plan.

The Maganzese themselves were better known than Ruggiero. No part of the tradition, not excepting the character and achievements of Orlando, was more definitely fixed or more universally notorious than the qualities and position of the clan of Maganza. Their real origin is to be found in Gan or Ganelon, the supreme traitor of Roncesvalles, to whom the *Song of Roland* attributes the defeat and death of its hero; though Ganelon was provided with ancestors as well as descendants in subsequent narratives as circumstances might require. Whatever their precise relation to Ganelon, every member of the clan shared in his disposition. One and all they were traitors and scoundrels, jealous, artful and irreconcilably hostile to the clan of Chiaramonte, to which Orlando, Rinaldo and others of the most popular Paladins belonged. Ariosto tersely describes one of their number as follows:

> Questo era il conte Pinabel, figliuolo
> D' Anselmo d' Altaripa, maganzese;
> Che tra sua gente scelerata, solo
> Leale esser non volse nè cortese.
> Ma ne li vizi abominandi e brutti
> Non pur gli altri adeguò, ma passò tutti.

> He was one Pinabel, a count, and son
> To Anselm of Altripa, Maganzese;
> Who in his scoundrel clan nor sought nor won
> A name unique for courteous gentilesse.
> But in all vices, and base, treacherous spite,
> Not only equalled but surpassed them quite.

> *Orlando Furioso*, II, 58.

A very different character was Archbishop Turpin, whose chronicle was the alleged source from whence Boiardo and Ariosto derived their information as to the doings of the Paladins. The chronicle actually existed, and perhaps was believed to be historical, though destitute in truth of all connection with Turpin of Rheims, the contemporary of Charlemagne; but the frequent appeals to its authority made by Boiardo and Ariosto are of course mere jest, designed in general to give emphasis to an absurdity.

Astolfo is one of the most important characters both in the *Orlando Innamorato* and in the *Orlando Furioso*, but traditionally he was not to be compared as a popular hero with either Orlando or Rinaldo. Exactly how far Boiardo's conception of his character is original it is perhaps needless to enquire; for whether original or not there is no difficulty in understanding it from the mere perusal of the *Orlando Innamorato*, apart from any other knowledge. Yet there may be one or two slight details which Boiardo takes for granted, as for example that Otto of England and Milone of Agrante were brothers, and Astolfo and Orlando consequently first cousins.

A number of other Paladins are mentioned in the *Orlando Innamorato* or in the *Furioso*, not all of them cursorily, but though in general derived from tradition, they may here be passed over without notice. Of the Pagan opponents of Charlemagne not much need be said. It is almost self-evident that the relations between the Emperor and the Saracens should be hostile, and that they or some of their allies should provide the vast armies which give opportunity for Orlando and other Paladins to exhibit their valour and skill in arms. The number of Pagans who are mentioned is very large, and many of them were traditional figures, but it would be tedious to attempt to trace the origin of names and details which have in many cases no great significance. The most conspicuous Pagan champions such as Rodomonte,

Mandricardo and Agramante are quite or very nearly original, and if Gradasso and Ferraguto may be considered exceptions, yet even here scarcely anything traditional is completely taken for granted, though many facts are mentioned in such a way as to show that they are assumed to be common knowledge. Thus Ferraguto is a Pagan champion of great valour and ferocity with a strong tendency to self-glorification. Like Orlando, he is enchanted so that he can never be wounded save in one part of his body and even more than Orlando he is deficient in personal attractions. His mother's name is Lanfusa, and she is a bitter and cruel enemy to all Christians. Serpentin and Isolier are his brothers. All these facts, and very possibly other details in addition, can be gathered from the mere reading of the *Orlando Innamorato* and the *Furioso*, but they were not new to Boiardo's audience, and he can bring them in where he likes without the risk of becoming unintelligible. This remark in truth applies more generally. Few essential facts are positively taken for granted with respect to either Pagan or Christian heroes but very many are introduced casually as familiar matters in no need of special explanation. Everywhere we are made to feel the traditional background which adds the weight of antiquity to much that would otherwise have been absurd or incredible even to the somewhat naïve tastes of Boiardo's readers.

Characters derived from the Arthurian legends are

naturally of very infrequent occurrence; for it would obviously have been impossible to bring the knights and ladies of the Round Table into direct contact with the Paladins of Charlemagne. Among the few may be mentioned Merlin and the fay Morgana; but though the garden of the latter plays a part of considerable importance in the *Orlando Innamorato*, she herself is a character of the utmost tenuity and vagueness such as scarcely to call for particular notice. The relative absence of names and characters of the Arthurian legends in the *Orlando Innamorato* and *Furioso* must not, however, at all be supposed to measure the debt of either Boiardo or Ariosto to this tradition. In his classic work on the sources of the *Orlando Furioso*, Professor Rajna has shown that in countless instances Ariosto has adapted Arthurian material to his own ends by changes of names and details which yet have not served, and probably were not intended, to conceal the origin of his conceptions. Doubtless if a like enquiry conducted with similar care and learning were made into the sources of the *Orlando Innamorato* it would reveal an analogous state of affairs; as indeed has in part been made clear by the researches of Razzoli and Bertoni. It is possible that this brief and imperfect outline has failed even to suggest the vast extent and variety of the romantic material upon which the *Orlando Innamorato* and the *Furioso* are, directly or indirectly, based; and perhaps has given to that material an

appearance of greater unity than in truth belongs to
it. On not a few points there were divergent tradi-
tions. The poems of Boiardo and Ariosto are extensive,
but the body of romance in prose or poetry exceeds
them by many times in bulk, and much the larger
part of it lies outside their scope. This world of
romance, the creation of several centuries of literary
labour, has now sunk into almost complete oblivion;
a few scattered names and incidents which have been
illuminated by the genius of some later writer being
all that most people know of the subject. In the
time of Boiardo and Ariosto that world was still
alive. Its characters and their adventures were still
familiar, and even its atmosphere, though more
subtle and evanescent, had not been wholly forgotten.
In real life, Bayard could still display without ridicule
much of the character, the sentiments and the actions
of a knight of romance. That this should have been
the case was an essential condition of the labours of
Boiardo and Ariosto. A vast world, even then
beginning to grow dim, was born again as the result
of their genius; but this new birth was no mere con-
tinuance of the older life; for they stamped upon
their poems the impress of their own personalities
and to some extent of the age in which they lived.
By so doing they enabled the world of romance to
maintain its existence through centuries when all
sympathy with mediaeval ideals and aspirations had
been well-nigh lost, and mediaeval thought seemed

merely pedantic and absurd. Our knowledge is certainly wider and our appreciation of past modes of thought and feeling perhaps more enlightened. On the other hand, every increase of knowledge adds to the number of competitors for our interest. When so much that is new is daily being brought to our notice the old is likely to be neglected. It will scarcely be denied that Boiardo and Ariosto have suffered from such neglect, at any rate in Britain. How far deservedly it would be futile to ask, for the relative valuation of works of genius must always be largely a personal matter. All that will be here attempted is to indicate the general character of the *Orlando Innamorato* and the *Furioso*, and to describe in outline the conditions under which they were produced. To do more than this would be to risk trespassing upon the prerogative of the reader.

II. Boiardo

THE family of Matteo Maria Boiardo, the author of the *Orlando Innamorato*, was ancient and noble. Alberto Boiardi, of S. Martino in Rio, not very far from Modena, is mentioned in a document of the year 1170, and two centuries later, the Boiardi, after various vicissitudes which it is unnecessary to detail, had gained the status of feudal nobility from the House of Este, to whom henceforth they remained unalterably attached, and in whose service more than one member of the family achieved distinction.

Feltrino Boiardo, the grandfather of Matteo Maria, attracted, at an early age, the favourable notice of Marquis Niccolo III, the slayer of Parisina, became his constant follower, and, after Niccolo's death, was a prominent figure at the court of his sons Leonello and Borso. He accompanied Niccolo on many of his frequent journeys, and transacted on his behalf much difficult and important business. His labours were not unrewarded, for in 1423 he was invested with Scandiano, Arceto, Torricella and Gesso, which six months later were separated from the territories of Reggio, and erected into a county, of which he became the first count. Finding the castle of Scandiano in ruins he speedily had it repaired, and held it with success during two years of war. It would have been difficult for anyone who was without a taste for letters to maintain his position at the court of the

scholarly Leonello, and Feltrino, though primarily a
man of affairs, was not untouched by the erudite
enthusiasms of the age. He was a keen if scarcely a
successful historian, and like his more famous grandson, attempted a translation of the *Golden Ass* of
Apuleius. When advanced in years he enrolled himself among the students of canon law at the newly-
refounded University of Ferrara, and three months
before his death borrowed from the library of the
Estense Augustine's *De Civitate Dei*.

In 1414, on the advice of Niccolo, he had married
Guiduccia Correggi, by whom he had several
children. He was an affectionate father, and was
overwhelmed with grief at the sudden and premature
death of his second son Pirro, a boy of much promise,
in 1446. By that date, Giovanni, the eldest son had
for some years been married to Lucia Strozzi. She
was one of the well-known Florentine family of that
name, and was a sister of Tito Vespasiano Strozzi,
almost the only genuine poet among the many who
wrote Latin verse at the court of Leonello, and
throughout his long life one of the most splendid and
conspicuous figures in the social world of Ferrara.
The birth of their eldest son, Matteo Maria, has
been generally supposed to fall in the year 1434,
from which it has been concluded that his parents
were married in 1433 at the latest. Giulio Reichenbach, however, has recently shown that this is a
mistake, and has proved by documentary evidence

that in 1439 Lucia was still unmarried. As she was unquestionably Giovanni's wife by 1442, and there are fairly conclusive reasons for believing that she was then a mother, the year of Matteo Maria's birth is fixed within tolerably narrow limits. Reichenbach inclines to the early part of 1441 on the grounds that Giovanni is known to have entered upon court service at Ferrara in the autumn of that year, while Matteo Maria speaks of Scandiano as his native place, and by an allusion in one of his poems makes it clear that he was born in the spring.

At Ferrara, Matteo Maria's childhood must chiefly have been spent until the death of his father in 1451, when he returned with his mother to his ancestral home. Feltrino was still alive, and efficient enough to have been appointed Captain of Modena in the previous year. He now took an early opportunity to resign this office, and returning to Scandiano, henceforth gave his chief care to his family.

In 1452 Duke Borso paid a visit to Scandiano. As the Duke was famous for his love of splendour, and Feltrino doubtless took pains that he should be received in an appropriate fashion, the incident must have made a strong impression upon the susceptible imagination of the future author of the *Orlando Innamorato*. Borso was accompanied by his half-brothers Sigismondo and Ercole. The last-named was the most striking personality of the three and won the whole-hearted and life-long devotion of

Matteo Maria, who was not very many years his
junior.

Four years later Feltrino died, leaving as his heirs
his only surviving son, Giulio, and his grandson,
Matteo Maria. In effect Giulio succeeded to the
authority of his father, but Matteo Maria had, as
yet, no cause to complain of the management of the
estate, for on his uncle's death in 1460 he wrote to
the Count of Sambonifacio: "It has been the
pleasure of the Creator to call to himself the blessed
soul of my good father Messer Julio, and as I have
been deprived of such a father you and my other
relations must be a father to me in his place." Giulio
was married to Cornelia Taddea Pio, of the family
of Pio of Carpi, and at his death left one son, by
name Giovanni. A few months later, Taddea gave
birth to a second son, who, according to the custom
of the time, was called Giulio, after his deceased
parent. At this date, Giovanni cannot have been
more than a child; for as late as the year 1483 we
find his mother writing on matters connected with
the property in her own name, and as if she were
absolute mistress of it. Matteo Maria not being
legally of age, the Duke appointed a competent
jurist to act as his guardian and administrator, and
as tutor to his cousins; a position which he still
occupied on the 28th of July, 1462. Humanism
was the fashion, and Matteo Maria (or Boiardo as
he may henceforth be called) received a good classical

education. His teachers were probably his grandfather, Feltrino, and the priest, Bartolomeo da Prato,
under whom his uncle Pirro had studied. The art of
writing Latin verse was being pursued with enthusiasm
by others besides Tito Vespasiano Strozzi at Ferrara,
and it is natural that Boiardo should have followed
in their footsteps. His earliest work appears to be the
Carmina which he wrote in praise of Ercole d'Este, and
the next, ten *Eclogues*, which, whatever their poetic
qualities, at least show a close acquaintance with
Virgil. He also attempted prose translations both
from the Greek and from the Latin. Among the
former are versions of Herodotus and the *Cyropaedia*.
Boiardo's knowledge of Greek was not adequate to
these tasks, nor did he make up by care for his
deficiency in scholarship. His Herodotus has many
mistakes, some of which reveal a failure to understand the sense of the original, and if the *Cyropaedia*
is at all better, this may be attributed to the fact that
here Boiardo made use of Poggio's Latin translation,
to which it is plain that he is largely indebted. It is
more surprising that his versions from the Latin
should hardly be marked by greater skill. He
treated the *Golden Ass* of Apuleius most cavalierly,
altering the conclusion, and in general showing so
little regard for accuracy that his work has rather
the character of an imitation than of a translation.
He nowhere reaches a high standard, though with
other Latin authors, as for example Cornelius Nepos,

he was more successful than with Apuleius. Such attempts are only of interest as witnessing to culture and intellectual tastes.

The library of the Estense was rich in French romances, which could, on occasion, be borrowed by their courtiers, and Bertoni has proved that Boiardo made good use of his opportunities in this respect, a circumstance which implies that in addition to Latin and Greek he must have possessed a competent knowledge of the French language.

For ten years after his uncle's death Boiardo lived quietly at Scandiano. He was never an ardent courtier and his home had many attractions. He was surrounded by beauties of nature of a kind to which he shows himself peculiarly sensitive. In some of the most characteristic descriptions of scenery in the *Orlando Innamorato* reminiscences have been traced of its author's native district. It is natural that little should be known of this period of Boiardo's life, but we may picture him as chiefly engaged with country sports and pleasures, local duties and the charms of literature and friendship. His generosity was proverbial, and he had frequent opportunities of proving his readiness to aid his humbler neighbours. Scandiano is at no great distance from Reggio, where Boiardo enjoyed rights of citizenship, as his father, grandfather and remoter ancestors had done before him. From the first his relations with his fellow-citizens were close and friendly; and, on their side,

the "Ancients" of Reggio were by no means blind
to the advantage of being able to appeal to so influ-
ential a man as Boiardo in any difficulty in which
their city was concerned. Among these the frequently
recurring disputes about the canal of the Secchia
were the most important. The works connected with
the canal had been begun, many years before, by the
Reggians, and had later been completed, on an improved plan, by Duke Borso. Injuries to this water
supply by accident or violence, attempts to use it for
private purposes, or to divert some portion of it for
the benefit of persons not belonging to Reggio, were
a source of constant anxiety to the "Ancients." They
knew that the waters of the canal were vital to the
prosperity of their city, and were always most jealous
of the slightest infringement of its rights. Boiardo
showed himself consistently helpful in this matter.
Several times he gave information of accidental
damage of one sort or another, and, on occasion, was
prepared to take, strong measures in support of the
city's rights. In 1473, when he heard that the Pii
of Carpi with a force of two hundred men were trying
to divert the waters of the canal to their own use,
he came down to Reggio and made a speech to the
"Ancients," defending their claims in the most
unqualified manner, and offering to maintain them
by law or by arms as might prove desirable. At an
earlier date he had shown that he was not careless of
his own advantage in the matter. A certain Simon

Calcagni began to construct works for the purpose
of using the waters of the canal to drive a saw mill.
Boiardo at once sent to destroy them, and justified
his action by the plea that Simon was trespassing
upon the lands of Scandiano.

The matter came before the Duke, who ultimately
left it to the Governor of Reggio for decision. The
Reggians, in their turn, were slow to oblige Boiardo
where the canal was in question. They imprisoned
a friend of his, by name Pietro Pernighetto, for dues
owing to the Commune on account of the canal, and
it required two letters from Boiardo, the second containing an offer to reimburse the city out of his own
pocket, before Pietro was released. The general
harmony between Boiardo and his Reggian neighbours was occasionally disturbed by other matters,
as for instance, in 1464, when the "Ancients" com-
plained that Rodolfo Grafagnino, who was known
to be on good terms with the Count, had carried off
some corn of theirs, and brought it to Scandiano.
Boiardo replied that on their own admission the corn
was not in Reggian territory, and concluded, "you
can regard the corn as being in your own market-
place since it is in my hands." Despite such trivial
causes of friction it is clear that Reggio owed much
to the friendship of Boiardo even before he was
appointed Governor, and that, on the whole, the
citizens were not unmindful of their debt.

In the year 1474 the even tenour of Boiardo's life

was broken by a serious family quarrel. Boiardo's aunt and elder cousin may long have viewed him with hostility, at any rate their interests were, in certain respects, opposed to his. No division of the estate between the cousins had yet taken place, and as Boiardo was still unmarried, Giovanni would, in the event of his death, succeed to all. On the 23rd of March, Antonio da Correggio writes to Duke Galeazzo Maria Sforza, and has a strange tale to tell, substantially to the following effect:

The wife of Lord Giulio (Boiardo) is the sister of Marco de Pii and the mother of Giovanni, and by what I have heard Marco de Pii and his sister have tried to have Matteo Maria poisoned by the help of a trusted servant and of his chamberlain. This servant, presumably repenting, determined to inform Matteo Maria, and was able to bring the sister of Marco to a place where Matteo Maria could overhear all the plan for poisoning him. It was agreed that with Matteo Maria's permission, the servant should go to get the poison from Marco, and bring it back to him. He did so accordingly, and Marco gave him the poison, which he brought to Matteo Maria, who took horse, and went with it to Duke Ercole at Ferrara, bringing his family and the chamberlain with him. When he got there he told the Duke everything. The poison was tested and found to be most venomous. Then the Duke sent for Marco de Pii, and he is at Ferrara. What will be done I do not know, but Marco is detained there. I have also been told that Matteo Maria has agreed with the Duke to exchange his lands near Reggio for some twice their value near Ferrara, and this is true

—which it was not for Boiardo refused the proffered

exchange—"The chamberlain was not Matteo
Maria's but Giovanni's, and it was he who arranged
the plot with the family." This letter of Correggio's
partly explains a letter written to Boiardo in the
previous February by the "Ancients" of Reggio, in
which they recommend to him (i.e. to his mercy)
Simone Boione, then in prison at Scandiano on a
charge of poisoning, and beg him to pass over the
whole affair. The "Ancients" met again on the
following day, and decided to send Pietro Antonio
Cassolo with a petition to the Duke, and another to
Boiardo, in which they beg the latter to give Cassolo
such a favourable answer as they would expect from
his clemency and kindness. There was good reason
for the warm interest that they took in the fate of
Simone Boione. His elder brother was a highly
respected official of Reggio, who was present at the
meeting of the Council when it was decided to write
to Boiardo, and who was doubtless mainly responsible
for the eagerness that the "Ancients" displayed in
the matter. Simone's was a capital offence, and he
was duly tried and condemned, but escaped the full
rigour of the law, and was merely sentenced to the
forfeiture of his property and banishment to Bagnolo,
which was, at that time, in the hands of the Gonzagas. The suggestion that Bagnolo was chosen as
the place of Simone's banishment because the Gonzagas were relations of Boiardo's wife has ceased to
be plausible since evidence has been found that he

was not married much before 1479. On the tenth of October the "Ancients" wrote again to the Duke, at Simone's request, begging him to annul the sentence of banishment. By this move they appear to have gained nothing, for in the next month we find them writing to Boiardo asking him to intercede with the Duke on Simone's behalf. It seems that Boiardo consented, for in 1475 Simone was again in Reggio, and in the enjoyment of an official position. On the death of the elder Boione, three years later, Simone succeeded to his office, and was a member of the Council of Forty when Boiardo was Governor of Reggio. In 1500 he was entrusted with the publication of the statutes, among which were some imposing the severest penalties on those guilty of the crime of poisoning. The Boionei had always been on good terms with Boiardo and we cannot tell what inducements were offered to Simone to engage him in the plot. The most likely explanation of the whole affair is that Marco Pio and his sister Taddea, with or without the knowledge and consent of Giovanni, were primarily responsible. As we have seen, Boiardo had lately supported the Reggians against Pio, and his property would pass to Giovanni on his death. Resentment and greed of gain are, at any rate, familiar motives for crime. The desire to hush up a family scandal would account for the slight penalty inflicted upon Boione, and for the reliance of the "Ancients" upon the intercession of Boiardo;

an intercession which, in view of the Duke's known friendship for him, was tolerably sure to prove effectual.

Sigismondo d'Este, the Duke's brother, held his court at Reggio, where Boiardo, as one of the chief local nobles and a devoted servant of the House of Este, must often have figured, in spite of his general distaste for a courtier's life. It was probably here that he first met and fell in love with Antonia Caprara, in whose honour were composed the lyrics which, next to the *Orlando Innamorato*, are Boiardo's chief title to fame. These lyrics were gathered together by Boiardo in his last years, and published, after his death, in three books each bearing the title *Liber Amorum*. They show that he fell in love in the month of April in the year 1469, when Antonia was about eighteen years of age. On the ground of references to youth and its follies, it has been supposed that some of these poems must relate to an earlier love, but this argument is deprived of most of its force when the date of Boiardo's birth is brought down from 1434 to 1441, and others to the same effect admittedly depend upon the interpretation of minute and ambiguous details. The conclusion that all the poems were addressed to Antonia Caprara is, in short, both the pleasantest, and by far the most likely. It may well be that Boiardo's sudden passion had, like that of Prasildo for Tisbina, its origin in a game. At first, it was returned by Antonia, but afterwards she became colder. There is, however, no need to attempt to follow the sequence of hopes and fears, meetings and partings, reproaches and rejoicings, jealousy and confidence which marks without distinguishing the course of Boiardo's love. His feelings were sincere and ardent, but of brief duration. In 1471 he accompanied Duke Borso to Rome. Absence does not appear to have diminished his love, but suddenly the note changes. Sad resignation takes the place alike of hope and fear. We are imperfectly informed as to what had happened. Antonia Caprara may have died. More probably, she was married to someone else. In any case Boiardo's love-affair was at an end, and Antonia passes out of his life. Most of Boiardo's biographers have stated that his own marriage to Taddea Gonzaga of Novellara speedily followed, taking place in the year 1472. Recent evidence suggests that by a curious coincidence Boiardo's marriage has, like his birth, been commonly antedated seven years. In a letter of March 15th, 1499, addressed to Duke Ercole, Taddea writes: "Dopo che io sono nella casa dello mio magnifico quondam consorte, che ora sono anni circa 19." This implies that she was married little if at all before 1480; and in another letter of July, 1479, she speaks of her marriage as quite a recent event. There is no record of her having any children before January, 1480. The marriage appears to have been a happy one, and in his will Boiardo speaks with respect and affection of his wife, and is careful to provide to the best of his power for her needs. Four daughters and a son, who died early, survived him, the estate ultimately passing to Giovanni. Another son was baptized in 1488, but as he is not again mentioned, he probably died in childhood.

Boiardo was warmly and sincerely attached to the family of Este and, in particular, to Duke Ercole. For him Boiardo wrote some of the translations already referred to, but his life was not destined to be one of lettered ease, and from a fairly early period, he was much engaged in the public service of the Duke. In 1469 he was among the gentlemen chosen to receive the Emperor Frederic III on his visit to Ferrara, and two years later accompanied Borso to Rome. With the accession of Duke Ercole in the same year his duties multiplied. He was one of the suite who brought the Duke's bride, Eleanor of Aragon, from Naples to Ferrara. Afterwards he held some office about the court, receiving in 1476 a salary of seventy lire a month, an amount exceeded by only one other official. In 1481 he was appointed Governor of Modena, a position both troublesome and important, remaining there until 1487, when he was transferred to the similar but more congenial post of Governor of Reggio. The nature of the duties which were imposed upon the governors both of Reggio and Modena may be gathered from the letters-patent which it was customary to issue, and of which some, dating from the time of Duke Borso, have been preserved. The Governor's salary was fixed at seventy-five lire a month, and he was to maintain at his own expense five horses and the same number of men, of whom three must be competent soldiers. He was to keep the keys of the city in his own hands, and see that the gates were opened and closed at the proper hours, that the captains of the gates kept good watch, and that they were duly paid their salaries every month. He was to meet the other officials in council at least once every day, and to arrange each month with the city treasurer for the regular payment of the soldiers, and make sure that these, in their turn, paid their debts. He was to settle disputes between the citizens and the troops, and, in case of bloodshed, had a limited power of inflicting punishment. The captains of the gates and of the fortresses in the city and district were under his orders. If it happened that some local baron wished to surrender his holding to the Duke, the Governor was to take possession of it without delay, unless he was engaged in the siege of some rebellious castle, in which case he was to await the orders of the Duke before moving. He was not to take military measures against villages or castles unless his authority had been set at nought; and he was strictly forbidden to accept gifts during his term of office. The character of these regulations suggests, what the letters of Boiardo fully confirm, that the Duke kept almost all real power in his own hands, and expected to be informed minutely of everything that occurred.

Boiardo made his official entry into Reggio on February 1st, and received a magnificent welcome from the citizens, chiefly, no doubt, because of his hereditary connection with the city, and the goodwill he had always shown towards it, but partly also by reason of his newly-acquired literary fame. In the previous year he had published the only two books of the *Orlando Innamorato* that were ever finished, that is to say about seven-eighths of the poem as we have it. They were an immediate success, and established his reputation as the greatest Italian poet of the age. Among his most ardent admirers was the Duke's daughter, Isabella d'Este, whose eagerness for the completion of the poem was perhaps sharpened by the expectation that it would de dedicated to her. It is not, in truth, very clear why Boiardo added so little to his work during the last years of his life. He breaks off quite abruptly with the famous stanza in which he laments the invasion of Italy by Charles VIII, and declares that under such circumstances he has no heart to continue the tale which he is telling. His grief was sincere and may even have hastened his death, but an invasion which took place in 1494 obviously does not account for the fact that he had composed no more than a few cantos since 1486. His slow progress is the stranger because there is good reason to think that the first two parts

of the *Orlando Innamorato* were complete, or nearly
so, by 1482, the year of the outbreak of the Venetian
War. Peace was made in 1484, and to this Boiardo
refers in the opening stanzas of his third book, where
he speaks of once more being able to take up his
tale now that the infernal tempest of war has passed.
As the unfinished book of the *Orlando Innamorato*
is in every way equal to its predecessors, we can only
suppose that advancing years, combined with the
labours and anxieties of his governorship, had deprived Boiardo of the energy for literary composition,
though not of his skill. In spite of his popularity
with the citizens of Reggio, his post was no easy
one. Reggio had suffered much during the war,
many had become demoralised and violence was rife.
The character of Boiardo's relations with the other
officials of the city made tact no less requisite than
firmness. Opinions differ as to how far Boiardo was
gifted with the latter quality. After his death,
charges of excessive humanity, resulting in the en-
couragement of crime, were made against him. We
have not a sufficient knowledge of the facts to
determine the justice of these accusations, but it may
well be that what many to-day would describe as
common humanity appeared blameworthy weakness
to those of the stricter sort in the sixteenth century.
One case illustrative both of the legal and social
conditions of the age and of Boiardo's disposition
may be quoted, and though we have no record that

complaint was made against him in this instance, we can easily imagine that there were those who disapproved of his conduct. Certain Jews were arrested on a suspicion of crime. The Duke assigned their trial to Boiardo, with a view to securing that any fines that might result should come into the ducal treasury. One of the accused, by name Vitale di Castelfranco, confessed to having had relations with a Christian woman. This was a capital offence, but Boiardo contented himself with imposing a fine of two hundred ducats. He informed the Duke of the matter, and told him that Vitale was very poor, and that if he could not pay he would be put to death; apparently meaning to suggest that the Duke would be wise to reduce the amount. The Duke gave the profits of the fine to one Alessandro, who is described as a captain of cross-bowmen, leaving him to exact as much or as little of the fine as he thought fit, and adding that the Jew really deserved death for such a crime. Boiardo, however, persuaded Alessandro to be content with sixty ducats. To raise even this sum Vitale had to borrow from four of his compatriots, and he was to be kept in prison until Alessandro had received the money.

Several times during Boiardo's governorship, the Duke sent Beltramino, a lawyer of Ferrara, to Reggio as his special commissioner with extensive powers, and with the not unnatural result that conflicts of jurisdiction arose between him and Boiardo which had to be referred to the Duke; a state of affairs which was not improved by the circumstance that Beltramino had a personal though hardly a reasonable grievance against Boiardo in connection with the place of residence to be allotted to the commissioner on his visits to Reggio. With other officials also, Boiardo's relations were sometimes strained, through no fault of his. More important and more troublesome than any of these matters were the consequences of Charles VIII's descent upon Italy. Duke Ercole had promised his son-in-law Lodovico Sforza to allow the French troops to pass through the territories of Ferrara, and to sell them provisions at a reasonable rate. The first soldiers to arrive were Italians in the service of Charles VIII. Boiardo was anxious that the provisions sold to them by the peasantry should be free of taxes so as not to raise the price, but the Duke refused to make any concession. Boiardo then suggested that the villagers along the line of route should be encouraged to bring their goods into the city, so that the soldiers, not finding provisions too abundant, should be led to hasten their passage through the Duchy of Reggio as much as possible. In the end, the Italians gave little trouble but the French who followed them were less manageable. Thefts and outrages took place frequently, and Boiardo was much distressed at the infliction of injuries which he could neither wholly prevent nor punish. On all these matters he wrote constantly and at length to the Duke, and it is noteworthy that amid all his labours he found time to give his master a minute description of the dress, manners and appointments of the French captain. Eventually Charles VIII decided on a change of route which relieved Boiardo from the burden of providing for these unwelcome guests. His anxieties told upon his health, and on October 5th he is recorded as being unable to attend the meeting of the Council of Reggio because of serious illness. He grew weaker during the autumn, his condition being perhaps aggravated by his failure to persuade the Duke to accept an offer of allegiance from the citizens of Fivizzano, a village just within the Florentine boundary which was exposed to the depradations of the French, and which was sacked by them towards the end of October. Although unable to attend the meetings of the Council, Boiardo continued to write to the Duke at frequent intervals upon public affairs. His last letter is dated November 22nd and on the nineteenth of the following month he died. In accordance with the terms of his will he was buried in the church of S. Mary in Scandiano. He directed that no one, save his wife if she should wish it, was to share his tomb. He left fifty gold ducats to S. Mary for the repair of the church. To the monastery of S. Mary he left 100 ducats and enjoined that if the monks were disposed to build a convent, his heirs should give them sufficient land for the buildings and a suitable garden. They were also to provide for masses to be said at the altar of S. Catherine three times a week at a cost of three hundred ducats. Legacies were given to several servants, amounting in one case to one hundred ducats. His wife was to have her dowry and five hundred ducats and to be the guardian of his son and daughters. To each of the four latter he left fifteen hundred ducats. His son Camillo was his heir with remainder to Giovanni and ultimately to Michel Boiardo of Ferrara. Larger and more careful provision was made for his daughters in the event of Giovanni succeeding, as actually happened; for Camillo died, childless, in 1499. Giovanni, however, evaded his obligations, a long drawn law-suit followed and at one time Boiardo's widow and daughters were in want of the necessaries of life, as we learn from a letter of Isabella d'Este's to her father in which she begs him to secure at least so much for them.

A year after Boiardo's death an edition was published of the *Orlando Innamorato* containing for the first time the unfinished fragment of the third book. The incomplete state of the poem was no bar to its popularity and fourteen other editions had followed by the year 1545, but it scarcely appears that Boiardo's family gained anything by his poetic reputation which before the last-named date had been overshadowed by the genius of Ariosto.

WHEN the Count of Scandiano began his famous poem the romantic tradition was, as we have already noted, in decay. The truth of this statement is scarcely affected by the circumstance that Luigi Pulci had published his *Morgante Maggiore* in 1482. The *Morgante Maggiore* is, no doubt, a poem of very considerable merit, but it is so individual, so full of its author's peculiar impish humour and so exactly suited to the tastes of his Florentine audience, that it was likely to have small vogue in other circles, and was ill-adapted to be the precursor of a general revival of romantic poetry. It seems, in point of fact, to have had no influence whatever upon the work of Boiardo, who may quite fairly claim the credit of initiating the special type of narrative poetry which, with considerable differences, was afterwards brought to perfection by Ariosto, and of having founded a poetic school, if a word so inappropriate to the temperament of Boiardo may be excused, which had more than one disciple of the most distinguished talent, and which profoundly affected the subsequent course of literature, not only in Italy but almost throughout Europe. Both in form and in matter, Boiardo is largely indebted to his predecessors of France and Italy, and yet his work is essentially original, with the unforced originality of genius which, conscious of its powers, does not disdain the use of common materials, however trivial or stale they may have proved in less capable hands.

Boiardo's task was made easier, and its character in part determined, by the fact that the current narrative poetry, though lamentably weak in all poetic qualities and scarcely deserving the name of literature, was, nevertheless, cast in a form which was excellently fitted to his purpose. The "ottava rima," originally a lyric stanza, had become the recognised medium of poetic narrative since the thirteenth century, if not earlier. Its advantages are so plain that even a foreigner cannot fail to observe some of them, though he must necessarily lack the refined perception of subtler beauties which belongs to those whose native idiom it is. The mere fact that it has been adapted to languages so unlike Italian as English and German, and has been extensively used by some of the greatest poets of both nations, is eloquent testimony to its qualities. It is light and rapid, and combines adequate length with compactness, so that it can mark off a single scene from its neighbours without having to cramp or distort its proportions. The final couplet is admirably suited either to emphasise a point, or to introduce an ironic comment, as occasion may require. Ariosto has shown to what brilliant account such properties as these may be turned in the right hands, and it would be unfair to deny to Boiardo a great, though not equal, power of making use of them. Apart from these advantages, the change of rhyme is useful in avoiding monotony, to which narrative poetry is much exposed.

The division into cantos was no less traditional than the stanza form. The point may seem trivial, and it might be objected that such division was not of enough consequence to be reckoned as an obligation which Boiardo owed to his predecessors, that all long poems are, of necessity, divided in one fashion or another, and the *Orlando Innamorato* among the rest. But the canto was not merely a division, it was a division with a specific character of its own; for it was, originally, as the word suggests, the extent of a day's recitation, and so far a distinct though not a separate entity. At the opening of each canto it was natural for the poet to refer back to the subject of the previous day for the benefit of fresh hearers, and at the close to give some idea of the next episode, in order to attract an audience for the morrow, while taking care to break off at a point which should leave curiosity still unsatisfied; behaving in short very much like the modern writer of stories for the newspapers; and for much the same reasons.

These beginnings and endings had normally a religious flavour; for, as Dante shows, the idea of writing for amusement, or from artistic motives, was unfamiliar to the mediaeval mind, which hankered after the instructive, or at least believed that it ought to do so. A few words of piety, which might be the merest form, were enough to satisfy this desire, and

to conciliate the goodwill of the priests, an indispensable requisite to any lasting popular success.
Boiardo drops the piety, but he preserves the form
of recitation; and may, in truth, have read his poem
aloud as it was being composed. Some few, at least,
of the opening lines in each canto are addressed to
his audience, and he turns to them again at the close,
though this latter break in the narrative is always
slight. The introductions are more elaborate, extend-
ing sometimes to several stanzas, and containing
general reflections, in the style which Ariosto was
to perfect, upon love, the instability of fortune, the
contrast between ancient and modern times and
similar topics. Boiardo's exordia are not so famous
as those of Ariosto, for few have any considerable
significance, but those few are as a rule of decided
merit. As a characteristic example, the following
may be quoted:

> Il sol, girando in su quel celo adorno,
> Passa volando e nostra vita lassa,
> La qual non sembra pur durar un giorno
> A cui senza diletto la trapassa;
> Ond' io pur chieggio a voi che sete intorno,
> Che ciascun ponga ogni sua noia in cassa,
> Et ogni affanno et ogni pensier grave
> Dentro ve chiuda, e poi perda la chiave.
>
> Et io, quivi a voi tuttavia cantando,
> Perso ogni noia et ogni mal pensiero,
> Et la istoria passata seguitando,
> Narrar vi volgo il fatto tutto intiero,

Ove io lasciai nel bosco il conte Orlando,
Con Feraguto, quel saracin fiero,
Qual, come gionse in su l' acqua corrente
Orlando il ricognobbe imantinente.

The sun, circling through the gorgeous heaven above, swiftly passes, bringing weariness to life, which seems indeed scarce to last a day to him who spends it without delight. Wherefore I ask you all to put your every grief into a box, and there shut up each trouble and each heavy thought, and then to lose the key.

And I have always lost in singing to you here each grief and painful thought, and wish to tell you all that chanced, continuing the story that I had begun, where I left Count Orlando in the wood with Feraguto that fierce Saracen, and how Orlando recognised him at once as soon as he reached the flowing water.   *Orlando Innamorato*, II, xxxi, 1, 2.

Boiardo's style is naturally much less crude than that of the popular romances, and is in many respects well suited to his subject, but it is not without serious faults. If it has much of the easy and un-affected character of speech, it is, likewise, apt to be tainted with provincialism; for Boiardo, being a Lombard, could not use the Tuscan with the un-conscious mastery of a Florentine. This particular defect, which is, of course, much more apparent to native than to foreign ears, had a decisive influence upon the ultimate fate of the poem. After enjoying great popularity for a time, it began to fall into oblivion as the reading public became more and more exacting upon the score of purity of idiom. Before

the middle of the sixteenth century it was super-
seded by Berni's *Rifacimento*, which in linguistic
quality was much better fitted to the taste of the day;
and when Panizzi published an edition of Boiardo's
Orlando Innamorato, in 1831, he was able to say with
truth that he was the first person who had thought
it worth while to do so for nearly three hundred
years.

Few foreigners can have so intimate an acquaintance with Italian as to be offended at Boiardo's de-
partures from the purity of the genuine Tuscan, but
some of his faults of style are more obvious.

Certain types of incident, such as battles and duels,
must recur with great frequency in romantic poems.
The danger of monotony becomes pressing, and the
repetition of very similar words and phrases hard to
avoid. Boiardo's imagination and command of
language were not always equal to this test. Epithets
such as "smisurato," "diverso" and rhymes such as
"taglia, maglia," "tempesta, resta," to name only a
few out of many possible examples, are repeated
again and again. Inadequate variety of rhyme and
phrase in adjoining or nearly adjoining stanzas is
occasionally noticeable. Instances are I, xvii, 11,
12, 15, and II, x, 34, 37, 38, and others more
striking might, no doubt, be found. In general,
Boiardo's language tends, not infrequently, to sink
towards the commonplace, and to give rise to the
feeling that though he may have selected a tolerably

good word or phrase, he has missed the best possible, the unexpected yet inevitable form, which Ariosto would have chosen under like circumstances.

These linguistic deficiencies must not, however, be supposed to counterbalance Boiardo's great and various merits, which have been more or less fully recognised by all competent judges since Panizzi rescued him from undeserved oblivion. A part of this reputation he owes to a bold and novel experiment. As we have seen, the romantic material upon which the *Orlando Innamorato* is based falls into two groups which have many points of contrast. Earlier authors had been content to choose one of the two great cycles of romance and to mould their work accordingly. Boiardo was more ambitious. Both the Carolingian and the Arthurian romances contained elements which he was unwilling to sacrifice. Would it not be possible to combine their distinctive qualities? Boiardo resolved to make the attempt, and produced the *Orlando Innamorato*. If Orlando was to be the hero, the framework of the poem must be Carolingian, and such a choice had certain obvious advantages. Orlando was the best known and most generally popular of all romantic characters. The world in which the Paladins moved was more spacious and varied than that of the Knights of the Round Table. Vast armies, commanded by mighty kings ruling over immense and distant territories, could be more naturally introduced, the scene could

E O

4

be changed at will to any part of the inhabited globe, and the feats of the chief heroes could be made more splendid and impressive. The Paladins were more distinct, closer to fact and less dream-like than King Arthur. Yet, in other ways, the Arthurian romances were better suited to the taste of Boiardo and his well-born audience. Their distinguishing characteristic was the predominance of the love-interest, with all that this implied. By depicting Orlando in love, Boiardo was able to combine the essential features of both types of romance, and to gratify the current taste for amorous scenes and sentiments. In so doing he was consciously breaking with tradition. Other Paladins might perhaps yield to passion, but not Orlando; least of all to a passion for an heathen enchantress, such as Angelica, the heroine of the *Innamorato*. He was the representative of mediaeval ideals, and among those ideals veneration for physical chastity had a leading place. He was the champion of Christendom whose life was absorbed in conflicts with the Pagan. Thus he was, first and foremost, a warrior of miraculous strength and prowess, and, though traditionally married, his marriage was one in name alone. When Boiardo wrote of Orlando in love, he repudiated this ideal, and put love in the place of religion as the supreme force in human life; a change consonant with that turning of interest from heaven to earth which marks the Renaissance. The point is of importance, and inevitably determined the character of Boiardo's poem in many ways, yet to emphasise it strongly might give rise to an entirely misleading view of Boiardo's temperament and aims. To suppose it part of his intention to disparage mediaeval ideals, and to substitute others for them, would be totally erroneous. He is quite free from serious purpose of any kind. He wished simply to amuse, and no settled principles informed, even unconsciously, his work. Love may be said to dominate the poem. If one was determined at any cost, to find some principle in Boiardo, one would find it in his belief in the irresistible power of love over all generous and noble minds. But even about love he is by no means too much in earnest. Orlando is very far from being a Tristram. Angelica has no resemblance whatever to Iseult, Guinevere or any such heroine of Arthurian romance.

The structure of the *Orlando Innamorato* reflects this absence of a central interest. It would be too much to say that it was devoid of plan. Its persons and incidents are connected, and its titular hero remains throughout the leading personage, though, if the poem had been completed, it seems not unlikely that his place would have been taken by Ruggiero in the last book, and that Angelica would have given way to Bradamante; as actually happens in the *Orlando Furioso*. It is perhaps not only in consequence of its unfinished state that the poem has no climax, but rather a part of Boiardo's method, and an expression of his peculiar aptitudes. His strength does not lie in the management of his fable as a whole, but in particular scenes and incidents. On these he lavishes all the resources of his fancy, and often with the happiest effect. He was dealing with themes and motives which were even then well-worn, but he succeeds in giving them freshness and vitality. Sir Walter Scott's romances illustrate the difficulty of making a good start, but it is a difficulty which does not in the least trouble Boiardo. His tale is better connected at first than it becomes later, and some of his most picturesque and entertaining scenes are to be found in the first few cantos of the *Orlando Innamorato*. Some account of these will serve to give the reader an idea of the substance of Boiardo's poem and of his method of treatment. Prefacing that its subject is Orlando in love, he mentions that Gradasso, the Pagan King of Sericana, is preparing to invade France, and then, in the eighth stanza, turns to describe the great tournament which Charlemagne is about to hold in Paris, and which really forms the opening scene of the poem. Many Saracens, as well as all the chief Paladins of the imperial court, are present. A great banquet has begun, and Charlemagne surveys with pride the magnificent spectacle, when an unexpected apparition produces universal astonishment.

> Però che in capo della sala bella
> Quattro giganti grandissimi e fieri

> Intrarno, e lor nel mezo una donzella,
> Che era seguito da un sol cavallieri.
> Essa sembrava matutina stella
> E giglio d' oro e rosa de verzieri;
> In somma, a dir di lei la veritate,
> Non fu veduta mai tanta beltate.

For at the entrance to the splendid banqueting hall appear four huge and fierce giants, and, in their midst, a damsel, followed by a single knight. She was like a morning star, a golden lily or a garden rose; in short to speak the truth of her, never was so much beauty seen.

Orlando Innamorato, I, i, 21.

It may be noticed, in passing, that the last two lines of this stanza illustrate the tendency to rather commonplace phrasing to which reference has been made. All gaze at her with equal surprise and rapture, not a Pagan but starts to his feet. The damsel explains that she is called Angelica, and that she has come with her brother, Uberto, from beyond the Tanais to take part in the Emperor's tournament. Uberto is waiting at the neighbouring Rock of Merlin, and is prepared to joust with any cavalier. If he is defeated, Angelica is to be the bride of the victor, but the vanquished become at once his prisoners, and must not attempt to continue the struggle on foot. Orlando, overwhelmed by Angelica's surpassing beauty, falls violently in love, and the other knights, both Pagan and Christian, are hardly less moved. One alone retains his self-command, Rinaldo's wise cousin, Malagise, who by his magic

arts discovers that Angelica's story is false, and that
she is, in truth, the daughter of Galiphrone, King
of Cathay, and has been sent by her father to entrap
the Christians. The danger is great, for not only is
Angelica herself a skilled enchantress, but her brother,
whose true name is Argalia, has been provided with
a magic lance of which the lightest touch will in-
fallibly unseat the most redoubted champion. Malagise determines to kill Angelica before it is too late,
but finding her asleep in front of her brother's tent
is turned from his purpose by the beauty of the sleeping maid, and seeks to embrace her, in the belief
that by necromancy he can prevent both his victim
and her attendants from waking. He is deceived.
Angelica is wearing a ring which counteracts all
magic, and immediately screams for help. Argalia
comes to her rescue and Malagise is taken prisoner,
and transported by demons of Angelica's summoning
to Cathay.

In the meantime, lots have been drawn for the
right to joust with Argalia, and fortune favours
Astolfo, the son of Otto, King of England. He is
duly captured and is succeeded by Ferraguto, who is
also overthrown, but refuses to surrender, alleging
that, as a Pagan, he is not bound by any agreement
that Charlemagne may have made about the terms
of the jousting. He and Argalia fight long, without
advantage on either side. Angelica despairing of the
issue, and seeing that, in any case, their plot is doomed

to failure, advises her brother to fly to the Ardennes, whither she will immediately follow him. Relying on the unparalleled speed of his horse, Argalia takes her advice and is hotly pursued by Ferraguto. Angelica summons her demons once more and vanishes in an instant, leaving Astolfo, who has been an interested spectator of these events, alone on the field of battle. Astolfo notices Argalia's lance, which has been forgotten in the confusion, leaning against a tree, and takes possession of it, though quite ignorant of its magic properties, because his own had been broken in the joust. On his way towards Paris, Astolfo meets Rinaldo and tells him what has happened, and that Angelica has fled. Without the loss of a moment Rinaldo sets off in pursuit. From the same source Orlando learns of Angelica's disappearance and Rinaldo's pursuit, and dreading the consequences, resolves to follow him as soon as night comes.

In spite of the departure of some of the most famous champions Charlemagne does not abandon the great tournament, and to it Boiardo now returns. The Pagan Serpentin enters the lists, prepared to meet all comers, but is finally overthrown by Ogier the Dane. Grandonio then takes Serpentin's place and triumphs over one Paladin after the other. It seems as if victory is to rest with the Pagans, but Astolfo's reckless courage and self-confidence make him willing to engage any opponent however terrible. Young and beautiful, nature has not endowed him with any special strength or skill, and all regard his defeat as certain, but Astolfo is carrying the magic lance, and Grandonio falls. Gano of Maganza, hearing of Grandonio's fall, enters the lists and offers, since there is no Pagan at the barrier, himself to meet Astolfo. Astolfo, who is at no time chary of words, replies:

> Va, rispondi a Gano:
> Tra un Saracino e lui non pongo cura,
> Che sempre il stimai peggio che pagano,
> De Dio nimico e d' ogni creatura,
> Traditor, falso, eretico e villano.
> Venga a sua posta, ch' io il stimo assai meno
> Che un sacconaccio di letame pieno.

Go, answer Gano that I make no difference between him and a Saracen because I always thought him worse than a pagan, an enemy of God and every creature, a false, heretic and cowardly traitor. Let him take his post, for I think far less of him than of an old sack full of dung.

Orlando Innamorato, I, iii, 13.

Gano and his followers are successively overthrown until one of them is bound to his saddle. The fraud is discovered and leads to a general scuffle. The Emperor intervenes personally, dealing blows right and left with his stick, breaking about thirty heads and loudly commanding his knights to abandon this unseemly strife. Astolfo is furious and pays no heed to Charlemagne's orders, who, at last, sends him to prison. With one of the abrupt transitions character-

istic of these romances, Boiardo now takes up the
story of the three knights who had followed Angelica
to the Ardennes. Rinaldo is the first to reach the
forest, and by chance drinks of a magic fountain
which turns his love for Angelica into hatred. Pro-
posing to return to Paris, he falls asleep by the River
of Love, which has properties exactly contrary to
those of the fountain. Angelica, drinking of the
river, becomes madly enamoured of Rinaldo whom
she discovers lying on the bank. She wakens him,
but he flies at once, and she is fain to pursue:

> E seguitando drieto li ragiona:
> Ahi franco cavalier, non me fuggire!
> Chè t' amo assai più che la mia persona,
> E tu per guidaron me fai morire!
> Già non sono io Ginamo di Baiona,
> Che nella selva ti venne assalire;
> Non son Macario, o Gaino il traditore;
> Anzi odio tutti questi per tuo amore.
>
> Io te amo più che la mia vita assai,
> E tu mi fuggi tanto disdignoso?
> Vòltati almanco, e guarda quel che fai,
> Se 'l viso mio te die' far pauroso,
> Chè con tanta ruina te ne vai
> Per questo loco oscuro e periglioso.
> Deh tempra il strabuccato tuo fuggire!
> Contenta son più tarda a te seguire.
>
> Che se per mia cagion qualche sciagura
> Te intravenisse o pur al tuo destriero,
> Serìa mia vita sempre acerba e dura
> Se sempre viver mi fosse mistiero.

Deh volta un poco indrieto, e poni cura
Da cui tu fuggi, o franco cavalliero!
Non merta la mia etade esser fuggita,
Anzi, quando io fuggessi, esser seguita.

And following after him she says: "Alas, brave knight,
fly not from me who love you so much more than myself!
And you for recompense would slay me! I am not Ginamo
of Bayonne coming to attack you in the wood, or Macario,
or the traitor, Ganelon; nay all these I hate for love of you.

I love you far more than my life, and do you fly from me
so disdainfully? Turn, at least, and see what you are
doing, and whether my face ought to make you afraid,
that you dash away from it with such fury through this
dark and perilous place. Stay your reckless course, I am
content to follow you more slowly.

For if by any fault of mine some accident should happen
to you, or even to your horse, it would always embitter my
life, yes, even if it were my fate to live for ever. Oh! turn
a little back, and see, fair knight, from whom you fly. It
fits not with my age that men should fly from me, but
rather that they should follow when I fly."

Orlando Innamorato, I, iii, 43–45.

Her appeals are vain. Rinaldo disappears from
sight, and lying down she, in her turn, falls asleep.

Here Boiardo breaks the thread of his tale to men-
tion that Gradasso has now arrived in Spain, and
then, going back to Ferraguto, relates how, meeting
Argalia in the Ardennes, he fights with him and
kills him. Orlando is not less fortunate than his
predecessors, for he discovers Angelica herself asleep
by the river bank. He forbears to wake her, and

stands gazing at her beauty, in wrapt admiration.
Ferraguto comes upon the scene, and immediately
fights with Orlando, and then Angelica awakes and
flies. Ferraguto refuses to suffer Orlando to follow
her, and the duel continues, until it is interrupted by
the arrival of Fiordespina, who comes with a message
to Ferraguto from Marsilio, King of Spain, praying
for his help against Gradasso. Ferraguto consents,
and Orlando, more courteous than his adversary,
raises no objection. Marsilio, though a Pagan, has
also appealed to Charlemagne, to whom he is related.
The Emperor entrusts the conduct of the campaign
to Rinaldo, who fights long and well-contested
battles with Gradasso. Finally, Gradasso challenges
him to a duel which is to take place the next
morning.

In the meantime, Angelica has been magically
transported to her native land, where she sets free
Malagise on condition that he persuades Rinaldo to
come to her. Rinaldo's hatred for Angelica proving
stronger than his affection for his cousin, he refuses
the proposal. Malagise, however, is not at the end
of his resources. A demon in the form of Gradasso
meets Rinaldo, and flying, entices him on board a
ship which carries him rapidly eastward. Rinaldo is
completely overcome by this catastrophe, and gives
way to his despair in heart-broken lamentations:

> Ah Dio del cel, dicea, per qual peccato,
> M' hai tu mandato cotanta sciagura?

Ben mi confesso che molto ho fallato,
Ma questa penitenzia è troppo dura.
Io son sempre in eterno vergognato,
Chè certo la mia mente è ben sicura
Che, racontando quel che me è accaduto,
Io dirò il vero, e non serà creduto.

La sua gente mi dette il mio segnore,
E quasi il stato suo mi pose in mano:
Io, vil, codardo, falso, traditore,
Gli lascio in terra e nel mar me allontano:
Et or mi par d' odir l' alto romore
Della gran gente del popol pagano;
Parmi de' miei compagni odir le strida,
Veder parmi L' Alfrera che gli occida.

Ah, God of Heaven, he cries, for what sin have you sent
me so hard a punishment? I acknowledge freely that I
have often been in fault, but this is too severe a penance.
I am put to eternal shame; for of this I am most certain,
that in telling what has befallen me I shall indeed speak
the truth, and yet will meet with no belief.

My Lord has trusted his men to me, has, one might say,
placed his fortunes in my hands, and I base, cowardly, false
and treacherous leave him on land, and seek the distant
sea. Even now I seem to hear the noise of the vast pagan
host, and the cries of my companions, and to see the
Alfrera slaying them.   *Orlando Innamorato*, I, v, 48–49.

There is no help for it. He is borne irresistibly
onward until he reaches an island palace with a lovely
garden.

Here we leave him and go back to Orlando, who
sets out for the East in pursuit of Angelica, and,

after various adventures, learns that she is besieged in
the castle of Albracca by the Tartar Emperor Agrican,
where he eventually joins her, meeting with many
strange accidents on the road. Of his adventures,
one may be mentioned as affording a characteristic
specimen of the touches of humour by which Boiardo
enlivens his tale. The dying struggles of a giant with
whom he has fought involve Orlando in an iron net
which he cannot break. The place is desert, and he
is threatened with death by starvation. A monk, who
afterwards shows himself exceedingly careful of his
own safety, appears and improves the occasion, exhort-
ing Orlando to patience, and continuing as follows:

> Molte altre cose assai gli sapea dire,
> E tutto il martilogio gli ha contato;
> La pena che ogni Santo ebbe a soffrire;
> Chi crucifixo, e chi fo scorticato.
> Dicea: Figliolo, il te convien morire:
> Abbine Dio del celo ringraziato.
> Rispose Orlando, con parlar modesto:
> Ringraziato sia lui, ma non di questo.

He knew many other things to tell him, and went over
the whole martyrology, the torture that each saint had to
endure, how one was crucified and another skinned. My
son, he said, it seems that you have to die, for which you
should have thanked God. Thanks be to Him, Orlando
humbly replied, but not for this.
>> *Orlando Innamorato*, I, vi, 20.

Throughout his tale Boiardo relies upon the traditional materials of romance, love, fighting, wonder

and the beauties of nature. It has been pointed out
with truth that "there is not a single note of mystery,
of the vague terror of the unseen, of the pathos of
man's struggle with supernatural elements, from the
first line to the last." Whether this is a defect is
a matter of opinion. Boiardo had no taste for the
intangible or the indefinite. He is not earnest
enough to wish to criticise, but accepts life as romance
pictured it, at its face value. He understands, and
can describe love, admitting without comment the
utmost extravagances of chivalry, but his view of
women is in reality that of Boccaccio, and he does
not even pretend to think them worthy of such
devotion. On the surface, at any rate, love is charm-
ing, and no true knight can be ignorant of its power.
After all he is only telling a tale. Why should he
run the risk of wearying himself and his audience
by attempting to go deeper? He adopts a similar
attitude towards the battles and duels which make up
a large part of his story. He was far from being
a pugnacious man, and was no religious fanatic.
Nevertheless, he affects to regard the battles between
Charlemagne and Agramante as the most important
and exciting parts of his poem because the slaughter
of vast hosts of Pagans was supposed to be magnificent;
and he does not care to quarrel with tradition on the
point. For like reasons, and for the sake of variety,
he introduces giants, magicians and fays with a free
hand, though he can have had little more belief in

their possibility than a modern man. Some of these
episodes had the additional advantage of enabling
him to give full scope to his powers of description.
He rejoiced in scenes of natural beauty, particularly
when they were gay and gracious rather than sublime,
apt to harmonise with marvellous products of human
art and wealth. Nature divorced from man, or in a
savage and hostile mood, makes little appeal to him,
but on nature as enhancing the beauty of human life
he lavishes all his poetic skill. The description of the
Garden of Falerina may be quoted as a favourable
example of this side of his genius.

> Era alla sua man dextra una fontana,
> Spargiendo intorno a sè molta acqua viva;
> Una figura di pietra soprana,
> A cui del petto fuor quella acqua usciva,
> Scritto avea in fronte: Per questa fiumana
> Al bel palagio del giardin se ariva.
> Per rinfrescarse se ne andava il conte
> Le mane e 'l viso a quella chiara fonte.
>
> Avea da ciascun lato uno arboscello
> Quel fonte che era in mezo alla verdura,
> E facea da se stesso un fiumicello
> De una acqua troppo cristallina e pura;
> Tra' fiori andava il fiume, e proprio è quello
> Di cui contava aponto la scrittura,
> Che la imagine al capo avea d' intorno;
> Tutto la lesse il cavalliero adorno.
>
> Onde si mosse a gire a quel palaggio,
> Per pigliare in quel loco altro partito;

E, caminando sopra del rivaggio,
Mirava il bel paese sbigotito.
Egli era aponto del mese di maggio,
Sì che per tutto intorno era fiorito,
E rendeva quel loco un tanto odore,
Che sol di questo se allegrava il core.

Dolce pianure e lieti monticelli
Con bei boschetti de pini e d' abeti,
E sopra' verdi rami erano occelli
Cantando in voce viva e versi queti.
Conigli e caprioli e cervi isnelli,
Piacevoli a guardare e mansueti,
Lepore e daini correndo d' intorno,
Pieno avean tutto quel giardino adorno.

Orlando pur va drieto alla rivera,
Et, avendo gran pezzo caminato,
A piè d' un monticello alla costera
Vide un palagio a marmori intagliato;
Ma non puotea veder ben quel che gli era,
Perchè de àrbori intorno è circondato.
Ma poi, quando li fu gionto dapresso,
Per meraviglia uscì for di se stesso.

Perchè non era marmoro il lavoro,
Ch' egli avea visto tra quella verdura,
Ma smalti coloriti in lame d' oro,
Che coprian del palagio l' alte mura.
Quivi è una porta di tanto tesoro,
Quanto non vede al mondo creatura,
Alta da diece e larga cinque passi,
Coperto de smiraldi e de balassi.

Upon his right a copious, sparkling fountain played,
carved of the finest stone in human form, and from its

breast the waters issued, and on its forehead were written the words: "To reach the garden-palace one must pass through this stream." The count approached the fountain to bathe his hands and face in its clear waters.

The fountain stood on a space of green, having on each side of it a little tree, and in front a rivulet of the brightest and purest water that flowed between flowery banks. This was the stream of which the writing on the figure told. The fair knight read it all.

Accordingly he set out for the palace, postponing until his arrival further decision; and as he walked along the river bank, he gazed with astonishment at the beauty of the scene. It was exactly the month of May so that everywhere the ground was covered with flowers, which gave forth so sweet a smell that that alone was enough to rejoice the heart. And that fair garden was full of sweet levels and gay little hills with pretty woods of pine and fir, and on their green branches birds were singing aloud their gentle song; rabbits and swift-moving stags, pleasant to see and tame, and hares and deer frisking around.

Orlando, however, kept by the river, and having walked for a great distance, came to the foot of a little hill, on the side of which was a palace with sculptured marbles, but what these were like he could not see for it was surrounded with trees; and when he came near he was beside himself with amazement.

For it was not marble that he had seen among those trees, but coloured enamels upon large sheets of gold which covered the high walls of the palace. Here was a door so rich that none had ever seen the like in the world; for it was ten paces high and five broad and was covered with emeralds and rubies.   *Orlando Innamorato*, II, iv, 20–26.

It has been noticed that there are touches in this

picture which are of Bretagne rather than of Italy, and reveal Boiardo's indebtedness to Arthurian sources.

In poetry composed of such materials the childishness of the fairy-story, and the commonplace of warlike feats performed by lay-figures, are both constant dangers, and Boiardo has difficulty in escaping them. He could not, as we have seen, depend upon the magic of style to cast a glamour over his materials, and their deficiencies must be plain unless he could find means to endow them with genuine interest and charm. Some might have found it possible to create out of them a world, which though, of necessity, different from the real world, was nevertheless coherent, vital and impressive; but to this task Boiardo's imagination was not equal. It would have implied that he was able to contrast the world of his fancy with the world of fact, and to recognise, at least in use, the principles which differentiated them; and for this he was not sufficiently an artist. His creations had not for him the vividness and coherence which would have allowed of his comparing them as a whole with reality; or, at any rate, he did not take his art quite seriously enough to sustain the attempt to do so. This carelessness, which from one point of view is a defect, perhaps contributed to enhance that air of freshness and light-hearted gaiety which is one of Boiardo's greatest merits. Of course all this is not equivalent to saying that he ignores the real world. To do that completely would have been to make a mere fairy-tale of the *Orlando Innamorato*, and fatally to limit the range of its emotional appeal. Explicit contrasts with real life are not frequent, but they are to be found. Such a contrast is expressed with great intensity in the famous and oft-quoted concluding stanza of the poem, where Boiardo feels that the horrors of the real world have broken in upon and for ever destroyed the gay world of his fancy. As a slighter example may be mentioned:

> Poi che quella arte degna et onorata
> Al nostro tempo è gionta tra villani;
> Ne l' opra più de amore anco è lodata,
> Poscia che in tanti affanni e pensier vani,
> Senza aver de diletto una giornata,
> Si pasce del bel viso e guardi umani,
> Come scia dir chi n' ha fatto la prova;
> Poca fermezza in donna se ritrova.

For in our time this noble and honourable art has fallen among men of base mind. Nor is the labour of love still praised, since one lives in so many troubles and vain thoughts from a fair face and kind looks, without having a single day's delight, as those can tell who have made proof of it; for little constancy is to be found in woman.

Orlando Innamorato, ii, xii. 3.

Situations which in feeling belong to real life are to be found more often. The despair of Rinaldo has already in part been quoted. The whole makes a still stronger impression of genuine passion; and it by no means stands by itself as evidence that Boiardo's lightness of tone did not at all prevent him from recognising and, on fitting occasions, making artistic use of the more powerful and serious emotions. His stanzas in praise of friendship, and his obvious affection for the Saracen knight, Brandimarte, the devoted friend of Orlando, have been justly cited by Mr Gardner as witnesses to the high value which he put upon this relation; and it may well be that Brandimarte represents more nearly the spirit of his creator than any other character in the poem. Even Angelica's love for Rinaldo is occasionally something more than a product of magic:

> Voi vi doveti, Segnor, racordare
> Di Angelica, la bella giovanetta,
> E come Malagise ebbe a lasciare;
> E giorno e notte stava alla vedetta.
> Or quanto gli rencresce lo aspettare,
> Sappialo dir colui che il tempo aspetta:
> Dico che aspetta promessa d' amore,
> Perchè ogni altro aspettare è rose e fiore.

> Ella guardava verso la marina,
> Verso la terra, per monte e per piano;
> Se alcuna nave vede, la meschina,
> O scorge vela molto di lontano,
> Lei, compiacendo a sè stessa, indivina
> Che dentro vi è il segnor di Montealbano;
> Se vede in terra bestia over carretta,
> Sopra di quella il suo Ranaldo aspetta.

> Et ecco Malagise a lei ritorna
> (E già non ha Ranaldo in compagnia),

Pallido, afflitto e con barba musorna:
Gli occhi battuti alla terra tenia;
Non ha di drappo la persona adorna,
Ma par che n' esca alor di pregionia.
La dama, che in tal forma l' ebbe scorto,
—Ahimè, cridava, il mio Ranaldo è morto;

You will remember, Sirs, the fair damsel, Angelica, and
how Malagise had to go away; and she remained night
and day upon the watch. Now how painful this suspense
was to her, he can best tell who awaits the time—I mean
who awaits the promise of love, to which all other waiting
is roses and flowers.

She looked towards the sea, and towards the land, over
the mountain and over the plain; and if she saw any ship
or distinguished any sail afar, the unhappy maid flattered
her hopes by guessing that it bore the lord of Montealbano;
or if, on land, she saw any carriage or beast of burden
upon which her Rinaldo could be.

And now Malagise comes back to her, and Rinaldo is not
with him. Pale he is, and sad and with disordered beard;
and he keeps his eyes fixed on the ground, and wears no
cloak, and seems as if he had just that moment come out
of prison. The maid, when she saw him in this guise,
exclaimed: Alas! my Rinaldo is dead!

Orlando Innamorato, I, ix, 2–4.

As might, perhaps, be expected Boiardo describes
the joys of love even more successfully than its pains
and anxieties. The meeting of Ruggiero and Bradamante on the battle-field, and the sudden growth of
their overwhelming mutual passion of which the
avowal is cut short by the attack of a body of Saracens,
form an episode which would be spoilt by any

attempt at general description, but it has long been recognised that in it Boiardo touches his highest point of lyrical feeling and shows himself capable of the truest poetry.

Orlando's grief when he sees Rinaldo's arms hung on the bridge, and believes him dead, is genuinely pathetic in its combination of tenderness for the long intimacy of the past with bitter regrets for their late quarrel which now can never be made up.

But it is not only to the softer emotions that Boiardo is alive. By far his most successful character, some would be inclined to say the only successful character, in the *Orlando Innamorato* is Astolfo; and Astolfo is essentially a humorist. Of his habitual extravagance of speech one example has been cited. He is everywhere a boaster but, far from being a coward, his unthinking self-confidence allows him to believe himself equal to any feat of chivalry, however dangerous, as when he goes out alone from Albracca to defy the whole army of Agrican. His natural generous vanity is heightened by the possession of the magic lance; for he, of course, attributes its results to his own skill. Astolfo is an Englishman, and though nationality has no particular meaning in romance, it is perhaps not altogether fanciful to trace national features in Astolfo's humour, self-confidence and bluff independence. It may be that there is here something more than a fortunate chance, and that Boiardo derived hints for the character of Astolfo from some of the Englishmen who studied under Guarino at the University of Ferrara.

Boiardo is a poet, but he is never inclined to put on the prophet's robes, nor is his humour restrained by any excessive regard for the alleged dignity of his theme. On occasion he does not spare Orlando; as in the description of his unattractive personal appearance and his awkwardness in love-making which do something to excuse Angelica's disdain. The knavish tricks of Brunello, the master-thief, are also related with obvious gusto.

Yet it is by no means upon the liveliness and truth of his character-drawing that Boiardo's reputation depends. On the contrary, this has very generally been regarded as one of the weakest features of his poem. This weakness has two sources. In the first place, the *Orlando Innamorato* is essentially a poem of action and adventure. Psychological romance was outside Boiardo's range. He was not interested in persons but in what they did. The visible world absorbed almost the whole of his attention, and it was therefore natural that if an action was striking he should not be careful to consider whether it was also appropriate to the person who was supposed to perform it, or consistent with the same person's behaviour at another time. Hardly conceiving of his poem as a whole, he felt little need for psychological harmony in the different parts. For example, Orlando is commonly thought to be one of Boiardo's most conspicuous failures in characterisation; yet the Orlando of any particular canto may be drawn with much force and truth. What is lacking is any thought for Orlando's behaviour at other times. He is by turns a theologian, a pattern of chivalric courtesy and a primitive, thick-headed paladin, not to speak of other rôles; and has, justly enough, been considered a different person in each canto.

This very absence of unity contributes to what is, perhaps, Boiardo's greatest charm, his unexpectedness. His fancy moves lightly along. There is no sense of effort, no single situation is allowed to become tedious, different incidents and emotions, the humorous, the wonderful, the pathetic and, occasionally, the horrible succeed each other in an easy and rapid flow, and carry the reader with them better than in many poems of greater pretensions to depth and force.

So elusive a charm is apt to evaporate in any attempt at illustration; but, nevertheless, it may be possible, by a fairly detailed study of one group of incidents, at least to suggest to the reader's mind the secret of this most characteristic quality. In the exordium to the first canto of the third book of the *Orlando Innamorato*, Boiardo describes, as we have already noted, how, the tempest of war being passed, he can at length resume his tale. He immediately introduces a new character, Mandricardo, the son of the Tartar Emperor, Agrican. Than Mandricardo no knight

was more courageous and more fierce, none more
skilled in arms or of greater strength, and none also
more proud and cruel. He ruthlessly puts to death
his own subjects if they lack strength and capacity
for war, until they fly the country in despair. One
old man is carried bound into the young Emperor's
presence, and begs that he may be heard; after he
has spoken they may do with him what they will.
"The soul of your father cannot pass into the infernal
regions, but must give way to meaner spirits; for his
death has been unavenged. Do you not know, or
do you pretend ignorance from fear, that your father
was slain by Orlando, who is unpunished, while you
are killing those who have done you no harm and
cannot defend themselves."

> Va, trova lui, che ti potrà respondere,
> E mostra contra Orlando il tuo furore.
> La tua vergogna non si può nascondere:
> Troppo è palese ogni atto de signore.
> Codardo e vile, or non ti dèi confondere,
> Pensando alla onta grande e il disonore
> Qual ti fu fatto? E sei tanto da poco
> Che hai faccia de apparire in alcun loco?

Go, find him who can answer you, and show your fury
against Orlando. Your shame cannot be hid, for every act
of a prince is too plain. Coward and base that you are,
ought you not to feel confused at the thought of the great
shame and dishonour that has been put upon you? And
are you so worthless that you dare to appear publicly in
any place?

Orlando Innamorato, III, i, 10.

Mandricardo is overwhelmed with anger, and immediately leaving the hall of audience shuts himself up in his chamber. He decides to abandon his kingdom, "Per non esser da altrui mostrato a dito" (a characteristic Renaissance touch), and vows never to return until his revenge has been accomplished. He provides for the government of his kingdom, places his crown in the temple of his gods and departs alone, unarmed and on foot; for he is too proud to owe even his armour to anything but his own efforts. Passing through Armenia, he comes to a little hill, and sees below him a lake, and close to it a tent, where he hopes to equip himself. He enters and sees arms upon the floor and a steed tied to a neighbouring pine. Up to this point we might well suppose that Mandricardo's revenge is really going to be the subject of the canto; but the situation now suddenly changes. No sooner has Mandricardo armed himself and mounted the horse than all around him bursts into flame. He dashes through the fire and hurls himself into the lake, but not before everything he has on has been consumed.

> E, mentre che a diletto il baron drudo,
> Per la bella acqua se solaccia e pesca,
> Parendo ad esso uscito esser de impaccio
> Ad una dama se ritrova in braccio.

And while the bold knight is swimming at ease through the water, in the belief that he has got out of the trap, he finds himself in a lady's arms.

Orlando Innamorato, III, i, 21.

The lady tells him that, like many others, he is a prisoner to the Fay of the Lake. Beyond the hill that he sees in front of him is a beautiful castle, and there are kept the arms of Hector which have come into the hands of the fay, all except the sword which Orlando won from Almonte. If he has the courage to face and overcome the enchantments by which they are guarded, he can gain these arms, and also set free himself and the many other knights who are the fay's prisoners. They leave the lake, and the damsel clothing him with her hair, they go together to the tent. Here Mandricardo finds arms, though not those of Hector, and sets out with his companion for the castle. The best of the previously captured knights, who, at this time, is Gradasso, King of Serica, has the duty of defending it against all comers. He and Mandricardo fight without advantage, until dragging each other from their horses they both fall to the ground, and Gradasso chancing to be undermost is declared vanquished. It is now evening, and to gain the arms of Hector Mandricardo must wait until the next morning, for the castle gates are always shut at night. The lady tells him that he can sleep where he is, or, if he prefers, she can take him to a palace where he will be welcome; but he will have to fight with a giant, which he may not care to do as he will have so much fighting on the morrow.

> Rispose Mandricardo: In fede mia,
> Tutto è perduto il tempo che ne avanza,

Si in amor non si spende, o in cortesia,
O nel mostrare in arme sua possanza:
Onde io ti prego per cavalleria
Che me conduci dentro a quella stanza
Qual m' hai contata; e farem male o bene
Se Malapresa ad oltraggiar ce viene.

Mandricardo replied: "In my belief, the rest of the time
is lost if it is not spent in love or in courtesy, or in showing
one's strength and skill in arms. Therefore I pray you in
chivalry to guide me to the place you have told me of: and
we will do what we can, be it ill or well, if Malapresa comes
to outrage us."   *Orlando Innamorato*, III, i, 52.

They are joyfully welcomed by the lady of the
palace and her damsels. Suddenly a hideous noise is
heard. The giant is breaking in. One might suppose
that Boiardo had been leading up to this as a climax.
But nothing of the kind. The giant is easily and
tamely slain.

Come se stato mai non fosse al mondo,
Di lui più non si fa ragionamento.
Le dame cominciarno un ballo in tondo,
Suonando a fiato, a corde ogni instromento,
Con voce vive e canto si iocondo,
Che ciascun, qual ne avesse intendimento,
Essendo poco a quel giardin diviso
Giurato avria là dentro il paradiso.

.   .   .   .   .   .

Ma qua non stette il cavallier lui solo,

Perchè una dama rimase a servire
De ciò che chieder seppe, più ni meno.

La notte ivi ebbe assai che far e dire,
Ma più ne avrà nel bel gioro sereno,
Come tornando potereti odire
Lo orrendo canto e di spavento pieno,
Che il maggior fatto mai non fo sentito
Adio, Segnori, il canto è qui finito.

Of him they spoke no more than if he had never existed.
The ladies began a round dance, playing on every sort of
instrument, both wind and string, and singing aloud so
joyfully that if anyone had heard it who was at a short
distance from that garden he would have sworn that within
was paradise.

But the knight did not remain there alone.

Because a lady remained to do for him anything that he
asked, neither more nor less. He had enough both to say
and to do that night, but he was to have more during the
fair and quiet day, as you will hear if you return and listen
to my song full of horror and fear; for never greater feat
was heard of. Good-bye, Sirs, the (day's) song is ended
here.   *Orlando Innamorato*, III, i, 63–66.

In the morning Mandricardo rides towards the
castle with his companion of the lake.

Ragionando con sieco tuttavia
De arme e de amore e cose dilettose.

Talking with her all the while of love and arms and things
delightful.   *Orlando Innamorato*, III, ii, 3.

The castle is open to all, but every knight who
enters must strike the shield of Hector which hangs
upon a golden pillar in the great court. As soon as
Mandricardo touches the shield the earth trembles,

the door by which he entered closes of itself, and at
the same moment another opens in front of him
revealing a field of corn, of which both the straw and
the ear are pure gold. Mandricardo's first task is to
cut this corn, and as he cuts it every grain turns into
some strange and fierce animal. The crowd of wild
beasts becomes more and more dense, and it seems
as if even his strength and courage were to prove of
no avail. He stoops, and by chance takes up a stone
which is endowed with magic properties, and throws
it among the animals, who straightway fall to fighting
with each other until they are all destroyed. Mandricardo then has to root up a tree, but as he strives
to do so the flowers falling to the earth turn into
noisome birds. At last he tears it up and from the
hole that he has made comes a great wind which
sweeps away his tormentors. Looking into the hole,
Mandricardo sees a serpent with ten tails which
comes forth to attack him. He strikes in vain, and
the serpent seizing him he falls into the hole from
whence it issued. In their fall the serpent's head is
crushed to pieces and Mandricardo is able to free
himself. He has no occasion to reascend for here he
finds the object of all his labours, the arms of Hector.
While he stands admiring them, he hears a noise, as
of the opening of an iron door, behind him and turning round sees a number of ladies, who enter dancing
together in couples, dressed in gorgeous and fantastic
garments, and proceed to arm him. He has reached

his goal and has for the present no more dangers to face.

Even the feebleness of an abstract can scarcely hide the strange charm of these adventures, more fantastic than a dream yet as precise and definite as the most tangible features of real life. But it may be asked if all this is anything more than a fairy-tale, more splendid, perhaps, than the general run of such tales, but not, in essence, different. The question is not impertinent, nor the answer entirely obvious. Boiardo and his contemporaries were in many respects highly civilised, they could hardly be called naïve, but neither the child nor the savage were forgotten. The pageant of life was irresistibly attractive to them, and the *Orlando Innamorato* is a many-coloured pageant. All that appealed directly to the senses was delightful, and of all their senses the eyes were the most eager and insatiable. In the adventures which have been just described, the predominance of the visible and in particular of joyous visions cannot fail to strike the reader. There are no shadows. Everything is in a clear light, and for the most part bathed in sunshine. The actual world was opening out before the men and women of that time in many undreamt-of ways. Much was really new, and more which had been previously unnoticed was now the object of lively interest, and had all the charm of novelty. Few institutions or beliefs seemed beyond the reach of change, and even sober men were chary of setting

bounds to the possible. Yet reality is always subject
to the ineluctable nature of fact and logic, and to the
passionate wills and teeming fancies of men all limits
were unwelcome. To the strong all things shall be
permitted, and no obstacle shall be beyond their
power to surmount. To the patient harvesting of
small gains and the careful loosening of Gordian
knots, men were little inclined. Difficulties there
might be. The more the better if courage, strength
and skill would suffice for an immediate and complete solution; for difficulties so conquered only increased the fierce consciousness of power. Boiardo
shared these instincts in some measure and to them
he appealed. He asks us to look, not to think; and
every kind of action that is intrinsically striking is
brought into play. He has little care for logic and
scorns the tame boundaries of fact, yet he is never
a dreamer for all must be distinctly imaginable or the
eye would remain unsatisfied. The vague, the confused, the dimly suggestive have no place. Neither
ethical nor even aesthetic considerations can be
suffered to impose bounds. All that is fitted to arouse
strong and vivid emotions can appear upon the stage
and must do so in its own person and unveiled. Even
sheer horror is pressed into service, as the story of the
Castle of Altaripa shows. Sex is universally interesting
and therefore Boiardo uses its motives freely. His
poem is not in fact licentious and there is nothing of
pruriency, or purity; but there are signs that here as

elsewhere he rejects limits, and it may well be that if he had lived to complete his last canto he would have afforded us unmistakable evidence of the fact.

The same spirit explains the love of marvels which almost turns Boiardo's poem into a fairy-tale. He piles wonder on wonder and multiplies dangers for his heroes to overcome because of gorgeous visions and the spectacle of victorious strength his fancy can never have enough. His profusion can be reckless, it is rarely unattractive. It has something of the abundance of life which may be rough, confused, and, at times, horrible, but is seldom merely trivial. It at least reminds us of Dryden's praise of Chaucer, "Here is God's plenty," though it is perhaps no more than a reminder. A fairy-tale cannot have these qualities; and they are sufficient to account for the charm which the *Orlando Innamorato* exercises over many readers.

IV. Lodovico Ariosto

LODOVICO ARIOSTO, the author of the *Orlando Furioso*, sprang from an ancient and noble family of Bologna. His ancestors can be traced back in the records of that city to the middle of the twelfth century, and were often very actively employed in the turbulent politics which were a main concern of life in Bologna, as in other Italian cities, during the age of the Guelfs and the Ghibellines. The connection of the Ariosti with Ferrara was due to chance. In the early part of the fourteenth century Obizzo d'Este, afterwards Obizzo III, Marquis of Ferrara, was an exile in Bologna, and falling in love with Lippa degli Ariosti made her his mistress. Their relations proved enduring. Lippa accompanied her lover on his return to his native city and bore him many children. In 1347, when she was on her death-bed, Obizzo married her, and three of her sons were successively marquises of Ferrara; of whom the youngest was the ancestor of all the subsequent princes of Este. Lippa drew many of her relations to Ferrara; among others Niccolo Ariosto, the great-great-grandfather of the poet, who became a citizen in the year 1363. The family prospered in their new home, and one or two of its members gave evidence of possessing literary taste and talent, while many of them held official positions under various princes of the House of Este. Niccolo Ariosto, the father of Lodovico, was a man of some

mark in his day. In the disputes as to the succession
to Ferrara which arose, after the death of Duke Borso,
between Ercole and Niccolo d'Este he took the side
of the former, and in 1471 was employed by him
to put a definite end to the matter by arranging to
poison Niccolo d'Este, who had taken refuge in
Mantua with the Gonzagas, his mother's relations.
Niccolo Ariosto duly succeeded in bribing one of
his namesake's servants to undertake the task, but
just before the time fixed for carrying it out, the
man was accidentally taken ill, and believing that he
had himself been poisoned, he confessed all, and was
executed.

Niccolo Ariosto escaped, and on January 1st of the
following year was appointed by Duke Ercole
Captain of the citadel of Reggio. He was paid the
large sum of 137 lire a month, but this was not a
personal salary, being almost wholly destined to the
support of thirty-two soldiers at the rate of four lire
a month each, so that Niccolo's own official remuner-
ation amounted to no more than nine lire a month.
In a letter to Duke Ercole he mentions that he had
been accused of starving these soldiers, presumably
with the intention of adding thereby to his gains.
He indignantly denies the charge, and declares that
he was in debt, and had spent out of his own pocket
more than fifty ducats. Whether there was any
foundation for the complaint we cannot tell; but
the Duke continued him in his office.

In 1473 Niccolo married Daria Malaguzzi, the daughter of a physician of Reggio who was also a minor poet. He had died in the year 1459, but he must have left a considerable property, for Daria received a dowry of a thousand ducats. In after years Lodovico was on excellent terms with his Malaguzzi cousins as is shown among other evidence by the fact that he addressed two of his seven *Satires* to Annibale Malaguzzi, and a third to Sigismondo. Lodovico was the eldest of ten children, five boys and five girls, and was born on September 8th, 1474, in the castle of Reggio.

In 1481 Niccolo was appointed Governor of the Polesine of Rovigo, but Rovigo being shortly afterwards captured by the Venetians, he returned, in November 1482, to Reggio. He had lost his property in Rovigo, and was without an official position, but he doubtless had other resources, and continued to live in Reggio as a private citizen until, in 1486, he was appointed Judge of the Twelve Sages in Ferrara. The appointment was not popular. It was rumoured that Niccolo owed it to a timely loan of 200 gold scudi that he had made to the Duke, and he was accused of the most remorseless theft and oppression in his new office. When Tito Vespasiano Strozzi was Judge of the Twelve Sages, a few years later, he is said, in spite of his literary distinction and apparent wealth, to have been "hated worse than the devil," so that it may be that the ducal officials

were generally disliked. In 1489 Niccolo became
Governor of Modena, and was succeeded at Ferrara
by one of the family of Trotti, who afterwards
proved themselves no friends to the Ariosti.

When Niccolo went to Modena, Lodovico remained
at Ferrara in order, by his father's wish, to study law
at the University under Giovanni di Sadoleto, one
of the professors. Lodovico tells us himself, in his
sixth *Satire*, that he had no taste at all for the law,
and he appears to have made indifferent progress
with his legal studies. It is said that Niccolo, having
occasion to pay a visit to Ferrara, gave his eldest son
a severe lecture on his idle and dissolute ways.
Lodovico listened to his father's rebukes without
attempting as much as a single word in his own
defence. His younger brother, Gabriele, who was a
spectator of the scene, was much impressed by his
senior's dutiful behaviour until, after their father had
left the room, Lodovico explained that he had not
interrupted the harangue because he wanted just
such an incident for a comedy that he was meditating,
and Niccolo was, unconsciously, providing him with
the most valuable copy. The scene which Lodovico
had in mind is to be found in his comedy *Cassaria*.

In 1494 Niccolo was persuaded to allow him to give
up the law and to follow his natural bent for literature.
Lodovico was already an author, for in the previous
year he had published an elegy on the death of the
Duchess of Ferrara, Eleanor of Aragon, and, as he

speaks of writing "in altro stil che in amorose tem-
pre," we may assume that this was not his earliest
composition. The inaugural oration to the University,
of which fragments can be traced in the first of his
Carmina, must be dated before 1495, and his ode
ad Philyroem probably in 1494, rather than in 1496.
If these dates are correct, it follows that the well-
known passage in the sixth *Satire*, where Lodovico
says that he was scarcely able to understand the
Latin translation of Aesop when past twenty years
of age, must be taken as a generous over-statement,
designed to enhance the magnitude of his debt to his
teacher, Gregorio di Spoleto, "whom reason wills
that I should always bless[1]."

Lodovico was one of a number of youths who went
with Duke Ercole to Pavia in 1493 to act in comedies.
This connection with Ercole, slight though it is,
perhaps does something to confirm the view of
Traversari that, contrary to the common opinion,
Lodovico was not beginning court service when he
entered the household of Cardinal Ippolito in 1503,
but that he had served Duke Ercole in 1499 and
1500, and possibly before and after those dates.

Whether this was the case or not, it is clear that
love and literature took up much more of Lodovico's
thoughts at this period of his life than courts or
politics. Of his love affairs not much is certainly
known, for he had a reputation for secretiveness in

[1] Che ragion vuol ch' io sempre benedica. *Satire VI*, 168.

such matters. In youth he was inspired by a passion
for a certain Pasifilia, and was at first unable to see
the true character of the girl and her relations.
Experience and the arguments of Bembo and other
friends were needed to convince him that Pasifilia's
mother was merely seeking to sell her daughter's
charms to the best advantage; a discovery which
plainly angered the youthful poet. Of other figures
who from time to time occupied Ariosto's "unstable
heart," and whose names are recorded in his *Carmina*,
such as Lydia, Ginevra, Glicera and Veronica, little
or nothing is known. Of more consequence was the
affair which led to the birth of his first son, Giovanni
Battista, about the year 1503. It has been generally
stated that Giovanni's mother was a family servant,
named Maria. This is a supposition of Ariosto's
biographer, Baruffaldi, and not an established fact;
but it is likely enough that the supposition is well-
founded. Giovanni became a soldier and had reached
the rank of captain when he died in 1569. He was
legitimated by Ariosto and inherited a small share of
his property. Another son, by name Virginio, was
born in the year 1509. His mother was a certain
Orsolina Catinelli da Sassomarino. Virginio, who
was his father's constant companion and his chief
heir, acquired some taste for literature. He has left
us notes on his father's character and habits, and
completed his unfinished comedy, the *Scolastica*; but
his work is lost, for the conclusion of the play as we

have it is due to Ariosto's brother, Gabriele. In
1514 Virginio's mother was married to one Mala-
cisio, and Ariosto gave her a dowry of six hundred
lire.

In the previous year Ariosto had paid his famous
visit to Rome to congratulate Leo X on his accession
to the Papacy, with the results that are described in
his third *Satire*. On his way back to Ferrara he
stopped for six months in Florence, and obtained
some consolation for his disappointed hopes of
advancement by falling passionately in love with
Alessandra Benucci, the wife of Tito Strozzi, a
small official of Ferrara, and a distant connection of
Tito Vespasiano Strozzi. Alessandra herself was a
Florentine, and related to Ariosto's friend, Niccolo
Vespucci. To her is addressed Ariosto's *Canzone*,
described as the finest Italian lyric of the sixteenth
century, in which he relates how he became the
captive of Alessandra on S. John the Baptist's day,
the festival of Florence, and "saw in all that fair city
no fairer thing than you." His love for Alessandra
was deeper than any that he had felt before, and
continued with undiminished fervour to the end of
his life. She was not young, having been born in
1480, but she was almost certainly beautiful, not
only in Ariosto's eyes but in fact, though all that we
know definitely of her personal appearance is that
she was very tall and had splendid golden hair. Tito
Strozzi died in 1515, leaving Alessandra with several

children of whom three afterwards became nuns. She was never publicly acknowledged as Ariosto's wife, for by marriage he would have forfeited a benefice that he held, and the relations between them are mainly a matter of inference, but there are strong reasons for supposing that they were in fact married by 1530 at latest, though they never lived in the same house. Of Ariosto's views on love and marriage in general it is possible to speak with more confidence than of his personal relations with women, for his fifth and longest *Satire* is wholly concerned with these subjects. It is addressed to his cousin, Annibale Malaguzzi. Ariosto has heard from others that Annibale is to wed but nothing from himself, and he suggests that the silence of the prospective bridegroom may be due to the fact that he thinks that Ariosto, being unmarried, disapproves of wives for others. If so he is quite mistaken, for:

I lament not having one, and excuse myself on the score of various accidents which have always prevented my goodwill from taking effect; but I was always of the opinion, and have said so many times, that without a wife at his side a man cannot be perfect in goodness. Nor is he able to live without sin, for he who has no wife of his own is forced to try and get one elsewhere by begging or robbing; and he who is in the habit of eating others' meat becomes greedy, and to-day wants thrush or quail and to-morrow pheasants or partridges. He does not know what love is or what is the worth of affection, and this is the reason why the priests are such a greedy and cruel lot.

Mi duol di non l' avere, e me ne iscuso
Sopra vari accidenti, che lo effetto
Sempre dal buon voler tennero escluso;
Ma fui di parer sempre, e cosí detto
L' ho piú volte, che senza moglie a lato
Non puote uomo in bontade esser perfetto.
Né senza si può star senza peccato,
Ché chi non ha del suo fuor accattarne,
Mendicando e rubandolo è sforzato.
E chi s' usa a beccar dell' altrui carne,
Diventa giotto, et oggi tordo e quaglia,
Diman fagiani, uno altro dí vuol starne.
Non sa quel che sia amor, non sa che vaglia
La caritate, e quind avvien che i preti
Sono sí ingordi e sí crudel canaglia.

Satire V, 10–24.

In addition to the usual grounds for not postponing marriage until old age, Ariosto urges the more characteristic objection that:

It is worse, he (ser Iorio) says, to see one in the cradle and two small boys playing about the house and a girl born a little before, and to have reached the limits of one's age, and not to have anyone, when one is gone, who will show them what is good and not defraud and despoil them.

Peggio è, dice, vedersi uno in la culla,
E per casa giocando ir duo bambini,
E poco prima nata una fanciulla,
Et esser di sua età giunto a confini
E non aver chi, dopo sé, lor mostri
La via del bene, e non li fraudi e uncini.

Satire V, 49–54.

Nor should he do as too many have done, who put

off marriage on the score of the expense of children, and are compelled at length to marry their low-born mistresses, "by which a great part of the good blood of Ferrara has been corrupted[1]." Love is blind, but if he is still capable of taking advice he will look carefully at the mother and sisters of his bride, for in character and habits she is likely to resemble her family. He will not seek too wealthy a wife who will cost him as much or more than she brings, but will be satisfied with one suited to his own fortune; nor will he look for exceptional beauty, for a beauty will be much sought after and will probably yield sooner or later.

Do not have one who is ugly, for with her you will have perpetual annoyance. I always praised the middle way and blamed extremes. Let her be of good mien and manner, one who does not sleep with her eyes open, for to be a fool is more disfiguring than any other evil blemish[2].

She should be modest and industrious and some ten years younger than her husband.

Let her fear God, but one who wants to hear mass more

[1] Quindi è falsificato di Ferrara
In gran parte il buon sangue,....

Satire V, 68, 69.

[2] Non la tôr brutta, ché torresti insieme
Perpetua noia: mediocre forma
Sempre lodai, sempre dannai le estreme.
Sia di buona aria, sia gentil, non dorma
Con gli occhi aperti, ché piú l' esser sciocca
D' ogni altra ria deformità, deforma.

Satire V, 169–174.

than once a day does not please me, and I think it quite
enough if she confess herself once or twice a year. I do
not wish that she should have much to do with the asses
who carry no burdens, and should every day make tarts
or pasties for her confessor.

> Tema Dio, ma che udir più d' una messa
> Voglia il dì, non mi piace, e vuo' che basti
> S' una o due volte l' anno si confessa.
> Non voglio che con gli asini che basti
> Non portano, abbia pratica, né faccia
> Ogni dì torte al confessore e pasti.

Satire V, 196–201.

She should not paint, nor would others wish that
she should do so, if they knew of what filth the
paints were composed.

He should treat his wife kindly, rebuking her when
necessary without anger, and never beating her; for
she is to be a companion and not a servant. He should
not keep her too much at home, for it is not in public
places that wives get into mischief; but he should
watch her without her knowing it, and remember
that if she wishes to deceive him she will certainly
succeed in doing so whatever his precautions, as an
old story proves.

The next *Satire*, in which he asks Cardinal Bembo
for advice as to the education of his son Virginio,
throws some further light on Ariosto's views, the
key-note being his insistence on the moral character
of Virginio's tutor as even more important than his
intellectual qualifications.

Ariosto was susceptible to friendship as well as to
love. In addition to his brothers and cousins, he had
many friends among those of his own age and standing
in Ferrara. Of such may be mentioned Alberto Pio
of Carpi, a young man of energy and promise who
afterwards became a bitter foe to the House of Este
and for this reason ceased to be on intimate terms with
Ariosto; and Ercole Strozzi whose mysterious assas-
sination in the streets of Ferrara has never been
wholly elucidated, the common opinion that the
Duke himself was ultimately responsible being far
from well-established. A closer friend than either
of these was Ariosto's connection Pandolfo Ariosto
who died young before he had made any mark in the
world, but to whose talent and merit Lodovico pays
a warm tribute, describing him as the flower of the
family. In 1498 began a friendship with the Venetian Pietro Bembo, the author, scholar and wit who
ended his life as Cardinal Bembo; a friendship which
lasted until Ariosto's death and does not appear to
have been at any time clouded by the far more
magnificent rewards secured by the lesser man.

All these friends had in common a taste for literature
and some degree of literary capacity, if Lodovico's
word may be accepted for Pandolfo in the absence
of more direct proof. Both Latin and Italian were
cultivated, but at this period Lodovico himself wrote
more in the former language and with greater success,
as Bembo's advice to him that he should continue

writing in Latin and not attempt a romantic poem
in Italian shows. It was of course never suggested
that he should write the *Orlando Furioso* in Latin,
though this has sometimes been asserted.

  The death of Niccolo Ariosto in 1500 put an end
to the pleasant life that Lodovico had been enjoying
in Ferrara. Niccolo, whether the charges of rapacity
which were brought against him were justified or
not, left a very moderate fortune, and there were
ten children to provide for besides his wife, who
survived him. His opportunities for gain had been
limited by his being out of employment for some
years before his death. In 1496, when Governor of
the Romagna di Lago, Niccolo heard that a certain
man had surprised his wife with a lover who had
fled leaving his cloak behind him. Niccolo sent for
the man and ordered him to produce the cloak. The
unfortunate husband refused and denied all knowledge of the incident. Niccolo then proceeded to
put him to the torture but without result, and the
matter coming to the Duke's ears he was dismissed
from his governorship and fined five hundred scudi.
He was never afterwards employed.

  Lodovico as the eldest son had now to take his
father's place and try to provide for his brothers and
sisters, some of whom were still quite young. He
left Ferrara and his books, and went to live on a
farm of his mother's near Reggio. His second
brother, Gabriele, was a cripple, and being unable to

engage in active life remained with Lodovico after the others had been launched on various careers, and attempted to follow in his footsteps as a poet. It has been suggested that he was the author of the *Rinaldo Ardito*, sometimes attributed to his more famous brother, and, as we have seen, he finished one of Lodovico's plays. Of the remaining brothers, Carlo became a soldier; Galasso, the recipient of the first of Ariosto's *Satires*, a priest; while Alessandro, the youngest, who was only ten years old at the time of his father's death, obtained a position as page in the household of Cardinal Ippolito d'Este, the brother of Duke Alfonso, and ultimately took orders. One sister married and two became nuns, the fate of the other two is uncertain.

In 1502 Lodovico was made Captain of the fortress of Canossa, but, as it was even then a ruin, his duties were probably not very arduous. A year later, he entered the service of Cardinal Ippolito as "familiaris." This position involved taking a share in entertaining the Cardinal's guests, and therefore brought him into close association with his master. Cardinal Ippolito was overbearing, violent and a lover of women, but he was not without capacity. His military talents were considerable, and some of his qualities appear to have excited genuine admiration. Castiglione, who had no very urgent reasons to covet the Cardinal's approval, thus describes him in the *Cortegiano*:

It is true that there are some who by the favour of the

stars or of nature are born with so much grace that it seems as if they were not born but that some god had fashioned them with his own hands, and adorned them with all advantages of mind and body....And to give you an example, you see Lord Ippolito d'Este, Cardinal of Ferrara, who has had the happiness that from his birth, his person, his appearance, his words and all his movements have been so graceful and so suitable that even among the oldest prelates (though he himself is but young) he exhibits so weighty an authority that he rather appears fitted to teach than to be in need of instruction[1]....

Ariosto's duties were by no means merely social. He was often employed in business matters, including some not unimportant embassies, and acquitted himself well. Nor was he wholly without military experience. He was under the command of Aeneas Pio di Carpi during the campaign which was marked by the victory of Cardinal Ippolito at La Polesella, and appears to have taken an active and creditable part in the second and smaller battle of the same name. He probably saw the field of Ravenna, though not as a combatant, and may well have had more direct acquaintance with war on other occasions.

Ariosto's poetic impulses were strong enough to overcome these obstacles. He perhaps began to think of composing a sequel to the *Orlando Innamorato* about the time that he entered the service of the Cardinal, possibly even sooner. The work progressed rapidly; for when sent on an embassy to Mantua at

[1] *Il Cortegiano*, i, xiv.

the beginning of the year 1507 to congratulate
Isabella d'Este on the birth of her son Ferrante,
Ariosto read her the earlier cantos with which she
expressed herself very greatly pleased. Two years
later he writes of the recent victories of Cardinal
Ippolito as affording him new matter for the decoration of the nuptial tent of Ruggiero and Bradamante
which is described in the last canto of the poem. As
the first edition was not published until the year
1516, this would seem to imply that Ariosto fixed
the plot and even many of the details of the *Orlando
Furioso* long before he had succeeded in giving it
a form which he thought worthy of publication,
thus displaying from the first that fastidiousness in
matters of style and language which led him constantly to alter and retouch his work up to the time
of his death. Shortly after the publication of the
Orlando Furioso, Cardinal Ippolito determined to go
to his bishopric in Hungary, and required Ariosto,
as one of his gentlemen, to accompany him. Ariosto
refused, to the great annoyance of the Cardinal, who
dismissed him from his service, deprived him of some
of the most valuable of the benefices that he had
given him, and, as far as we know, never admitted
him to his presence again. This incident has led many
to suppose that Cardinal Ippolito was entirely blind
to the literary genius of his servant, but this is,
perhaps, to do him an injustice. He paid the expenses
of publishing the first edition of the *Furioso*; and we

have no reason to think that he was so devoid of
artistic perception as to believe it without merit; but
he was proud and passionate, and likely to hold that
any behaviour that did not happen to be convenient
to him, or any resistance to his will, was an unfor-
giveable offence in such a man as Ariosto. For a
short time Ariosto attempted to live on his own
private resources, but they were obviously inadequate
even to his very modest needs, and in 1518 he
entered the service of the Cardinal's brother, Duke
Alfonso, at a salary of twenty-five lire a month.
Alfonso was perhaps the less trying master of the two,
but Ariosto frankly confesses that all court service
is distasteful to him, and would clearly have preferred
to live independently if this had been possible.

The *Orlando Furioso* was an immediate and striking
success; but however greatly it may have contributed
to Ariosto's fame it brought him very little profit,
and he had no choice but to remain with the Duke.
At the time he may well have expected to be relieved
from his servitude before many years had elapsed, for
his cousin, Rinaldo Ariosto, was a man of wealth,
and Lodovico was his natural heir. Rinaldo in fact
died in the year 1519 and Lodovico duly took
possession of his estate. He did not, however, enjoy
it for any length of time, for it was at once claimed
as crown property by the Duke's agent, Alfonso
Trotti. Ariosto appealed to the Duke against this
injustice, but without effect, for he was merely sent

back to Trotti. From a petition addressed to Duke Alfonso after Lodovico's death it appears that Trotti had some personal animus against the poet. On one pretext or another he prolonged the litigation indefinitely. The petition was as fruitless as the other efforts of the Ariosti to obtain a settlement, and the property long remained in the hands of the Estense, passing finally to the Jesuits. The anxiety and disappointment connected with this affair are said to have embittered Ariosto's life and to have robbed him of the energy for literary composition. At about the same time he suffered financially from other causes. War deprived him of his share in the receipts of the Chancellery of Milan, and also made impossible the payment of his salary as a member of the ducal household. Even when peace was restored, matters did not much, if at all, improve. At length the poet frankly declared that things could not go on as they were, and that if the Duke could do nothing for him, he would be compelled to try and push his fortune at some other court. Alfonso's own tastes were scientific rather than literary, but he was well aware that it would have been universally considered disgraceful if a man of Ariosto's fame and genius had been driven by poverty from Ferrara.

A convenient opportunity of meeting the poet's demands soon presented itself. The remote and mountainous district of the Garfagnana, originally belonging to Lucca, had come, for the most part, into the hands of the Estense, but during the recent war had been occupied by Florentine troops. On the death of Pope Leo X a successful revolt had taken place, and the rebels had appealed to the Duke of Ferrara to appoint a Commissary over the Ferrarese portion of the district, a request to which Alfonso eagerly consented; all the more so because the emoluments of the Commissary were not to be paid by himself but by the three vicariates into which the Garfagnana was divided. He offered the post to Ariosto, who reluctantly accepted it. The salary was good, amounting to fully three times what he was nominally receiving from the Duke, but in other respects the appointment was little to his mind. The task before him was a difficult and thankless one. The natural features of the Garfagnana were not very favourable to a civilised state of society, and the political disturbances of the last few years had contributed further to demoralise many of the inhabitants. Ariosto had also personal reasons for discontent. He disliked leaving his friends and the amenities of life in Ferrara, he disliked and feared both travelling and mountains, he would have few opportunities for literary work, and he would be separated for long periods from Alessandra. He had, however, practically no choice and in February, 1522, he set out with a heavy heart for Castelnuovo, the capital of his district. Much the greater part of the surviving correspondence of Ariosto consists of letters to the

Duke and others relating to the affairs of the Garfagnana during his tenure of office and this accidental
circumstance has perhaps tempted some of his biographers to attach greater importance to this period
of his life than it really deserves. When we remember
that Ariosto was by this time nearly forty-six years of
age, it becomes incredible that his residence in the
Garfagnana should have had any considerable influence on his character, though it doubtless afforded
him an opportunity of displaying qualities that might
otherwise have been unknown to us. His main duty
was to restore some degree of order, and to suppress
the bandits who were rife in the district. If he was
not wholly successful, he is scarcely to be blamed,
though he says himself that "He was not the man
to govern others, for he had too much pity and had
not the nerve to deny what was asked of him[1]." His
administration does not, however, appear to have been
conspicuously weak. His measures for checking the
bandits were well contrived. He secured the punishment of several prominent criminals, and would have
achieved more in this direction if he had been adequately supported by those with whom he had to
work. With the authorities both of Lucca and of
Florence he had constant difficulties, which he
laboured hard, and not quite fruitlessly, to surmount.
It was nearly two years before the compact for the
mutual surrender of bandits which Ariosto suggested

[1] *Campori Lettere*, x.

within a few months of his arrival at Castelnuovo, was agreed to by the "Ancients" of Lucca. Of a similar compact with Florence Ariosto complains that though he observed it the Florentines did not. Even his own Duke was not always helpful. At the beginning of the year 1524 Ariosto writes:

If I condemn or threaten those who disobey me and then your Excellency absolves them, or settles the matter in a way which shows that you favour them rather than me... it would be better to send another magistrate[1].

And he then goes on to cite instances in which the Duke has believed others in preference to himself. In this case Ariosto's appeal was successful; and that the Duke was not dissatisfied with his capacity may be inferred from the fact that, whether officially or otherwise, he had the refusal of the post of Ferrarese ambassador at Rome from the ducal secretary, Pistofilo. On the other hand, the Duke had taken no notice of Ariosto's wish to be transferred to the more congenial governorship of the Romagna, and this may perhaps indicate that his talents were diplomatic rather than administrative. Our information is scanty but on the whole we may conclude that Ariosto was a tolerably capable Commissary who, in a position where complete success was impossible, did as well as any man could have done who was averse from the very drastic forms of violence by which a temporary improvement in the con-

[1] *Campori Lettere*, XL.

dition of the Garfagnana might perhaps have been effected.

In 1525 the Duke accepted his resignation and he returned to Ferrara. He was eager to take seriously in hand the revision of the *Orlando Furioso*, a task which occupied much of his time during his later years. To it he was now able to devote himself with little interruption, for though he was still one of Alfonso's gentlemen, his duties were light. Shortly after his return from the Garfagnana, he bought a small cottage with a garden in Ferrara, and a year afterwards he divided the family property with his brothers, and went there to live. The change was presumably made with a view to giving him more leisure for his literary work. Ariosto, however, was not merely the author of the *Orlando Furioso*, he was also a dramatist of considerable merit and more reputation. His interest in the theatre at Ferrara was keen. For it he wrote several of his comedies, and designed the fixed scenery which was one of its greatest glories, the scenery of a theatre being considered so important that even Raphael did not disdain to paint one. In November, 1531, Ariosto was sent on a diplomatic mission to the Marchese del Vasto, who was then at Correggio, and from him he received an annuity of a hundred ducats, in consideration of course of his literary abilities and not of his diplomatic work. In the following year Alfonso went to Mantua to meet Charles V, and

Ariosto accompanied him. The Emperor may be presumed to have received the poet with favour, for in his final edition of the *Orlando Furioso*, Ariosto inserted verses expressive of the warmest admiration for his genius and beneficent activity; but the story that he was crowned laureate by Charles is a mere fable.

Ariosto's health had never been good. His digestion was weak, and he had long suffered from what he describes as catarrh, in a severe form. When he returned from Mantua he was obviously failing, and the destruction of the theatre by fire, on the last day of the year 1532, gave him a shock from which he never really recovered. His ill-health, which appears to have been a form of consumption, steadily increased, and on July 6th, 1533, he died. He is reported to have declared himself not unwilling to die, and to have said that if it were true that men knew their friends beyond the grave it seemed to him a thousand years until he rejoined those whom he had lost.

The bulk of his small property was left to Virginio, but he also made provision for Alessandra and, to a rather slight extent, for his eldest son, Giovanni Battista. The inference that Ariosto was comparatively indifferent to Giovanni's welfare is, however, highly precarious. A capable soldier in such times of almost incessant war may well have been able to provide very adequately for himself. The main features of Ariosto's character are plainly revealed in his *Satires*, in the biographical notes of his son Virginio and in the allusions of other contemporaries; but Ariosto was a reserved man, and the intimate touches which distinguish the portrait of an individual are scantily known to us. He was not, as a casual reading of his great poem might suggest, a man of impulse and uncontrolled imagination. His apparent artlessness is really a product of the most careful art, and it is plain that he was of a reflective and rather melancholy disposition. His most authentic likeness, the woodcut prefixed to the edition of the *Orlando Furioso* published in 1532, gives perhaps an exaggerated impression of gloom. It represents Ariosto in his old age, and when he was worn by sickness. In earlier life, he must have been less cadaverous, and may have been more cheerful. It is even possible that the well-known portrait in the National Gallery which goes by his name is genuine, though the weight of opinion is against it.

His was essentially a kindly nature, averse from inflicting, and, it may be added, from bearing pain or hardship. One of his strongest passions was the love of independence, but honour and affection proved themselves stronger. For the sake of his brothers and sisters he bore the burden of court service, highly distasteful to him as it was. His sacrifice was not made in vain, for all the family of whom we know anything made careers for themselves in the world, and seem to have repaid Lodovico with their affection. To many his extravagant flattery of Cardinal Ippolito has seemed the most serious blot on his character, all the more because we learn from his second *Satire* how little basis it had in his real feelings. His honesty in money matters has long been unquestioned. It is clear that with regard to the family property he behaved with honour and most probably with generosity, though details are naturally unavailable. In his official capacity as Commissary of the Garfagnana he was free from reproach. Accusations, whether justified or not, against the characters of prominent persons were far from rare, nor was official corruption and rapacity by any means extraordinary, and the fact that no such charges were ever made against Ariosto may therefore be taken as a tolerably conclusive proof of the actual purity of his administration. In this respect his character might be pronounced without the slightest blemish if it were not for a document of the year 1517, which records his acceptance of a bribe of ten ducats from a certain Bernard in order to secure that a case in which the said Bernard was interested should not come before a particular judge. As we know nothing further of the circumstances it is hard to estimate the degree of Ariosto's turpitude, but when full allowance has been made for the current standards of honour, the document in question is evidence that Ariosto was not altogether so scrupulous in pecuniary matters as

has been generally supposed, though it is certainly
not by itself sufficient to destroy his claims to be a
man of honour. Ariosto was a poet but he lacked
some of the qualities traditionally associated with the
art. The key-note of his character appears to have
been a cool, kindly but not uncritical good-sense. He
did not expect too much either of life or of his
neighbours, and was probably by no means blind to
the faults even of his friends, warm as his affection
for them was. We may judge him variously but
the judgment of his contemporaries was uniformly
favourable, and this he may have owed in part to a
certain simplicity and absence of vulgar ambition.
He set less store by externals than many, and was
a man of simple habits free from ostentation and
content with modest pleasures. In the race for the
prizes of the world men had little to fear from him.
In misfortune they had something to hope from his
kindness of heart. Such a character makes few
enemies in life and deserves none in death.

THE *Orlando Furioso* is admittedly one of the great poems of the world, yet it does not appeal to every competent judge; nor would it be difficult to name critics of eminence whose unwilling approval reveals, as clearly as their censure, that neither the poem nor its author have succeeded in winning their affections or arousing their enthusiasm.

The grounds for this distaste are many; but one at least, and that perhaps the most important, is, though often unexpressed, not far to seek. To many people poetry is a substitute for philosophy. Finding formal philosophy too arid or too abstruse, they turn to poetry for the satisfaction of their philosophic questionings, and of that vague, but often powerful, emotion which the spectacle of life and the universe awakens in reflective minds. Many students of philosophy are in like case; for being inspired by the same emotional needs, they find in poetry more than philosophy is able to give. It is not possible that the *Orlando Furioso* should make any over-mastering appeal to such persons. Ariosto's point of view, like every point of view, has its philosophical implications, but the charm and value of his poem depend upon what it is, and not upon what it suggests or implies.

As a highly distinguished foreign critic has said:

All these stories of Ariosto's, all the figures that pass before our eyes, are nothing but themselves, and fulfil their purpose in being products of art. For Dante poetry was the teaching of wisdom in the guise of allegory. Renaissance art represented reality for its own sake, and on account of its beauty, and not for the sake of any hidden symbolic meaning.

A like contrast, but perhaps even more fundamental, exists between the *Orlando Furioso* and *Faust*, the most representative poetic achievement of the modern mind. Though the meaning of *Faust* is in many respects obscure, some of its most important character-istics are plain to every reader. It is clear that Goethe wishes to suggest more than he distinctly expresses, that *Faust* is a vehicle for conveying to the world the repercussion of a long and varied experience of life upon his own personality, that this experience has for him an universal significance, which he aims at embodying, partly in ideas, but chiefly in poetic imagery and symbol; nor is it less evident, that his purpose was not, and, from the nature of the case, could not be completely achieved, since it was an attempt "to express in imagery or ideas that which in its fulness, and by its contrasts, bursts through every fixed form." In the *Orlando Furioso* there is nothing of all this. Ariosto is nowhere struggling with unmanageable material which it is beyond his power to shape. He has no philosophy of human life that he wishes to teach; for though his ideals are visible enough, he has neither moral system nor didactic purpose. His work reflects his personality but conscious self-revelation plays no part in it; and he has no vague depths to suggest, for he is a poet and not a philosopher and does not affect to have any key to the riddles of human existence. Both *Faust* and the *Orlando Furioso* occupied the attention of their authors for a great number of years, but the causes of this prolonged labour were quite different. As late as 1830 large parts of *Faust* were still unwritten, and scenes upon whose importance Goethe himself dwells were ultimately omitted. Nothing in the composition of the *Orlando Furioso* really corresponds to this. Ariosto never ceased working at it, and was notoriously dissatisfied with the edition of 1532, the last published in his lifetime; yet the six additional cantos and the innumerable minor alterations which distinguish it from the edition of 1516 do but enhance the general effect, and give increased brilliance and purity to the style. Even as early as 1509 the scheme and some of the details of the poem were, as we have seen, so far determined that Ariosto could refer specifically to matters belonging to the last canto.

Apparent similarities of subject in *Faust* and the *Orlando Furioso* likewise cover, without concealing, profound differences. Both Goethe and Ariosto are much indebted to the classics, but not in parallel ways. Both make use of symbol and allegory but with very unlike aims and results. In *Faust* the symbolism is vital, the story, save for Gretchen, nought. From the *Orlando Furioso* every trace of symbolism and allegory could be eliminated without great loss, and the most definitely symbolic episode, that of Ruggiero and Alcina, owes none of its undoubted merits to this feature, and almost reads like an attempt at instruction which was condemned by Ariosto's maturer judgment and thenceforth abandoned.

Faust, especially in the second part, is crammed with Greek names and allusions, but of substantial borrowings, whether of persons or incidents, there are few. Goethe was not concerned with fact, mythological or historical. He wished to show what the Hellenic spirit meant to him, and what, in his view, it ought to mean to humanity; and the rather wooden and self-conscious Olympianism of his later life was the result. Ariosto borrowed from Greek and Latin story with a much freer hand, seeing the many beauties of the classic myths, and using them without stint for his own purpose. But he had no desire to become a copy of an ancient Roman. He was free from pedantry and was less blind to the defects of the older civilisation than some of his contemporaries. It would be tedious to pursue further the analogies and the contrasts between the *Orlando Furioso* and *Faust*, which have served their turn if they have at all contributed to define the general character of the former; but of Ariosto's debt to the classics something more must be said. Carducci and others have pointed out how vitally Ariosto's study and practice of Latin affected his Italian, by chastening its exuberance, smoothing away its initial roughness, and giving it a measure and proportion that had previously been wanting. An influence of this kind almost eludes illustration, which could, in any case, only be attempted by a master of both languages, and perhaps only by one to whom Italian was native; but to forget its magnitude would be to misapprehend fundamentally the genesis and nature of the *Orlando Furioso*. The risk of such forgetfulness is, however, diminished by the number and extent of Ariosto's specific obligations to his favourite Latin authors.

Professor Rajna's epoch-making work on the sources of the *Orlando Furioso* proved that Ariosto hardly wrote a canto without drawing upon his store of classical knowledge. Virgil, Ovid, Catullus and Lucan, to name only the chief, made rich contributions, lending not merely phrases or casual details, but the most material parts of many and important episodes. Illustration is so easy as to be almost superfluous. The mutual relations of Cloridano and Medoro and their night-attack on the Christian camp are manifestly borrowed from the episode of Nisus and Eurialus in the ninth book of the *Aeneid*, though Ariosto has heightened the effect by making the prime motive Medoro's ardent desire to recover the corpse of his lord, Dardinello. Bireno's desertion of Olympia recalls the well-known story of Theseus

and Ariadne, and Professor Rajna has traced in it
detailed analogies to many passages of Catullus and
Ovid. The funeral of Brandimarte corresponds to
the obsequies of Pallas in the eleventh book of the
Aeneid, and the sea-fight between Dudone and
Agramante has been compared with, and, indeed,
thought superior to that between Brutus and Domitius
in Lucan's *Pharsalia*. The story of Perseus and
Andromeda was paralleled in the first edition of the
Orlando Furioso by the rescue of Angelica from the
Orca by Ruggiero, where his magic shield plays the
part of the Gorgon's head, and was repeated, with
considerable variations, in the edition of 1532, where
Orlando saves Olympia from the same monster.

These scenes could not easily be excelled for brilliance and vigour by any in the poem. There is no
hint of the languor which might be expected in an
imitation, no awkward hiatus revealing the imperfect
junction of original and borrowed matter. Everything is adapted to its context, and to the atmosphere
of the poem as a whole, and with such consummate
taste and skill that most readers would be inclined to
question Ariosto's dependence upon classical sources,
if the fact were not entirely indisputable. In every
requisite of style Ariosto displays an equal mastery.
His difficulties were great. The *Orlando Furioso*
includes, as we have seen, matter of the most various
origin. It is very long, comprising nearly five
thousand stanzas; and change and movement being

essential, new figures and scenes are constantly introduced, and make the task of preserving throughout a coherent plan and harmonious tone well-nigh impossible. Being also the product of long years of labour, and subject to the most meticulous revision, one might expect to find magnificent and rare patterns of carefully chosen words, beautiful, perhaps, but here and there over-handled and showing marks of the file. It would be easy to name acknowledged masters of language to whom some such description would apply. It has in point of fact no application whatever to Ariosto. Grace and lightness without the faintest hint of strain or affectation are his most salient characteristics. That Ariosto is simple is less obvious, but no less true. He has not simplicity of every kind. The construction of his sentences may sometimes be complex, and bold inversions for the sake of euphony or like advantages of style can easily be found; though page after page is perfectly straightforward. Neither are his words always simple; for his vocabulary is vast, and may be said to embrace all the resources of the Italian language, albeit there is a noticeable avoidance of conventional poetic phrases. Yet Ariosto is simple, because the most essential quality of his mind required simplicity. Art reached its zenith in his lifetime, and his own perceptions had the vividness and accuracy that belong to a painter. Every scene is a picture, so clear as to be visible to the dullest imagination.

He is pictorial even to a fault; and Lessing has cited
his description of the beauties of Alcina as an example
of the too close assimilation of poetry to the plastic
arts. Happier instances abound, as the awakening
of Olympia:

> Nessuno trova: a sè la man ritira:
> Di nuovo tenta, e pur nessuno trova.
> Di qua l' un braccio e di là l' altro gira;
> Or l' una or l' altra gamba; e nulla giova.
> Caccia il sonno il timor; gli occhi apre e mira;
> Non vede alcuno. Or già non scalda e cova
> Più le vedove piume, ma si getta
> Del letto, e fuor del padiglione in fretta;
>
> E corre al mar, graffiandosi le gote,
> Presaga e certa ormai di sua fortuna.
> Si straccia i crini, e il petto si percuote:
> E va guardando (che splendea la luna)
> Se veder cosa, fuor che 'l lito, puote;
> Ne, fuor che 'l lito, vede cosa alcuna:
> Bireno chiama; e al nome di Bireno
> Rispondean gli antri che pietà n' avieno.
>
> She no one found; the dame her arms withdrew;
> She tried again, yet no one found; she spread
> Both arms, now here, now there, and sought anew;
> Now either leg; but yet no better sped.
> Fear banished sleep; she oped her eyes; in view
> Was nothing: she no more her widowed bed
> Would keep, but from her couch in fury sprung,
> And headlong forth from the pavilion flung,
>
> And seaward ran, her visage tearing sore,
> Presaging, and now certain of her plight:

> She beat her bosom, and her tresses tore,
> And looked (the moon was shining) if she might
> Discover anything beside the shore;
> Nor save the shore, was anything in sight.
> She calls Bireno, and the caverns round
> Pitying her grief, Bireno's name resound.
>
> *Orlando Furioso*, x, 21, 22.

Less strictly pictorial but of like vivid effect is Aquilante's meeting with Martano:

> Pensó Aquilante al primo comparire,
> Che 'l vil Martano il suo fratello fosse;
> Che l' ingannaron l' arme e quel vestire
> Candido più che nievi ancor non mosse;
> E con quell' oh che d' allegrezza dire
> Si suole, incominció; ma poi cangiosse
> Tosto di faccia e di parlar ch' appresso
> S' avvide meglio che non era desso.

> Sir Aquilante believed at the first show,
> His brother he in vile Martano spied,
> For arms and vest, more white than virgin snow,
> The coward in the warrior's sight belied,
> And sprang towards him with that joyful "Oh!"
> By which delight is ever signified;
> But changed his look and tone when nearer brought,
> He sees that he is not the wight he sought:
>
> *Orlando Furioso*, xviii, 78.

Ariosto's realistic exactness often approximates, like an overwhelmingly cogent proof, to humour, as in *Orlando Furioso*, I, 76, where Sacripante's behaviour is precisely that of a man who having just escaped being kicked by his horse is still feeling anger not unmixed with fright.

It would be presumptuous in a foreigner to attempt judgment of the subtler harmonies of language or of the unfailing tact with which Ariosto is said to have preserved all the sweetness and grace of the purest Tuscan without any sacrifice of strength, and to have shaken himself free from pedantic reliance on accepted models without falling into provincialism. On such points he must be content in the main to receive the opinion of Italians, who are unanimous in affirming that for perfection of style Ariosto has few equals and no superiors among the world's poets. Yet even a foreigner can scarcely fail to recognise the music and the exquisite aptness to the scene of such lines as:

> Quel di' e la notte e mezzo l' altro giorno
> S' andò aggirando, e non sapeva dove:
> Trovossi al fin in un boschetto adorno,
> Che lievemente la fresca aura move.
> Dui chiari rivi mormorando intorno,
> Sempre l' erbe vi fan tenere e nove;
> E rendea ad ascoltar dolce concento,
> Rotto tra picciol sassi il correr lento.

> One day and night, and half the following day,
> The damsel wanders wide, nor whither knows;
> Then enters a deep wood, whose branches play,
> Moved lightly by the freshening breeze which blows.
> Through this two clear and murmuring rivers stray:
> Upon their banks a fresher herbage grows;
> While the twin streams their passage slowly clear,
> Make music with the stones and please the ear.

Orlando Furioso, I, 35.

The beauty of the whole is not less than that of the separate parts, and is as much distinguished by rapidity, ease and grace. The poem is like some swift and clear stream flowing through a brilliant and variegated landscape, chequered by its light and shade, but preserving in every situation its own peculiar loveliness.

But style alone is not sufficient. "The consummate expression of nothing" is not the task of genius. A supreme poem must have besides qualities of style an adequate subject and a degree of structural unity corresponding to the nature of that subject. We must, however, be careful not to exaggerate the scope of these requirements. The love of system belongs perhaps more to the critic than to the artist. If other examples were lacking, Byron's *Don Juan* would be enough to prove that an essentially trivial and commonplace theme together with an absolute minimum of structural unity is compatible with high artistic achievement. The dignity of poetry, like the dignity of history, has often been most loudly proclaimed by the incompetent prig. Yet when full allowance has been made for these considerations, we can scarcely deny that a subject appealing to the stronger and more vital human emotions, and possessing a unity of form which, though variable within wide limits, must involve something more than the simple juxtaposition of practically independent scenes, is needful if a supreme work of art is to emerge. At first sight Ariosto has failed to satisfy either of these requirements. The *Orlando Furioso* has several leading themes, but no one of them is so distinctly predominant as to be the indisputable subject. To some the love of Ruggiero and Bradamante, to others the madness of Orlando, and to a few perhaps the conflict between Charlemagne and Agramante, will seem respectively entitled to the position. The difficulty is not due to the inherent character of Ariosto's materials. Each of the topics named might have afforded a fitting subject for a masterpiece of poetry. The story of the chequered but finally successful love of Ruggiero and Bradamante has all the elements of romantic comedy, if the note of passion were appropriately stressed. Similarly the madness of Orlando in consequence of his vain love for the pagan princess Angelica is clearly a tragic theme, contains even as it stands genuinely tragic features, and might have been used to give the poem an essentially tragic interest; and finally, the world-embracing strife between Charlemagne and Agramante is of the stuff of which historical dramas are made. Nor does this use of dramatic terminology at all imply that in order to become any of these things the *Orlando Furioso* must have ceased to be a narrative poem. Ariosto might easily have cast his work in one of these moulds, though in fact he adopted none of them.

The reason why Ariosto never felt that there was

any need to group the matter of his poem around a single subject which should form the centre of interest and give unity to the whole is not very hard to divine. He was before all things an artist. The love of beauty for its own sake was his dominant passion, and it was natural for him to express it by making beauty itself the unifying principle of his poem. There is in the *Orlando Furioso* something more than the beauty which is present in every successful work of art. It is, of course, true that in literature many things that are not in themselves beautiful may be turned to aesthetic account; though whether the aesthetic value of tragedy is beauty in the same sense as we speak of the beauty of a picture or a landscape is perhaps a question more easily asked than answered. In any case it is clear that there are tragic or pathetic scenes, such as, for example, the blinding of Gloucester, or Mrs Mackenzie's nagging torture of Colonel Newcome, which no one ever read to the end and then exclaimed how beautiful! as might easily happen with art of a different quality.

The appeal of tragedy is highly complex. In all literature, and perhaps in all art, the enjoyment of loveliness is consciously accompanied by other emotions. The penumbra of feelings and associations which, however dim, are yet actual parts, and not merely causes or conditions, of the aesthetic state of mind almost defies analysis. It may be that in tragedy the equilibrium in which some have found the most

characteristic element of beauty is wittingly disturbed
for the sake of intensifying one, or a particular
group, of emotions; and the result shows that we
often think the sacrifice, if it exists, fully justified.
But this does not seem to apply in an equal degree
to all arts. Few of the great pictures of the world
represent suffering; and the apparent exceptions,
such as Michelangelo's "Last Judgment," are of the
sort that prove the rule, for there the suffering is
supposed to be the fiat of perfect love and perfect
justice; and analogous explanations would hold of
other religious pictures. Ariosto lived in an age of
great painters, and his conception of beauty had much
likeness to theirs. Beauty was not dependent only on
the form imposed by the artist. The initial character
of the material that it was sought to mould was not
indifferent to him. His was an essentially critical and
reflective temperament and he was not likely to over-
look any limitations that might logically be implied
by his aesthetic instincts. He was no mystic "with
the mystic's sense of unity and infinite peace and his
absence of indignation or protest, his acceptance
with joy and his disbelief in the ultimate truth of the
division into two hostile camps." He could never have
written with approval as Dante wrote

> Io son fatta da Dio, sua merce, tale
> Che la vostra miseria non mi tange
> Ne fiamma d'esto incendio non m' assale.

I am made such by God, in his grace, that your misery

does not touch me; nor the flame of this burning assail
me (CARLYLE).   *Inferno,* II, 91–94.

His Latin education, confirming what nature had
begun, gave him a characteristic sense of measure,
and made chaotic impulse and blind gropings after
some ineffable loveliness that none can firmly grasp
alike impossible to him. The true subject of beauty
is elusive and may well include the contemplator as
well as the contemplated; but without attempting to
penetrate further into the mazes of aesthetic philosophy, we may be content to affirm that in Ariosto's
view some only among objects were beautiful, and
that he aimed at making these the sole constituents
of his poem, while the part of the mind, whatever it
may be, in the production of aesthetic values had
little interest or meaning for him.

Whether right or wrong, his decision limited the
scope of the *Orlando Furioso,* and gave it a unity,
which if not of the most obvious kind, is clearly
perceptible to the attentive reader. This may seem
equivalent to the admission that the essence of the
Orlando Furioso is, after all, to be found in something
distinct from what it directly expresses, that it is, so
to speak, symbolic of the spirit of beauty; but such
an interpretation would be incompatible with what
has been said as to the objective and thoroughly un-
mystical character of Ariosto's mind.

The dominance of a principle does, however, imply
that Ariosto conceived of his poem as a whole, and

not merely as a succession of gorgeous fragments. Many critics have, no doubt, thought otherwise, and with much apparent justification. Ariosto's materials were not of a kind to fall readily into a simple pattern, and it was his aim to conceal rather than to emphasise the seriousness of his aesthetic purpose. In a sequel to the *Orlando Innamorato* he must seem to be spending with unstudied profusion the treasures of a boundless fancy, and his consummate art enabled him to give this effect to what was in truth the product of great care and labour. Nevertheless both the structure and the substance of his poem reveal a method different from that of his predecessor. A close analogy may be observed between the poems of Boiardo and Ariosto and the works of contemporary painters. It is well known that the beginning of the sixteenth century witnessed a vital change in the character of Italian art. A very competent critic has said that it was the aim of the Italian painters of the fifteenth century,

To give to the surface of the picture as rich and various a decoration as possible, using small, delicate forms and clear colours, under, as far as might be, equal illumination …with the consequence that such pictures can be divided into fragments and still sold to advantage.

This description applies with curious exactness to the *Orlando Innamorato*. But the same critic has pointed out that the artists of the next age adopted a different method, that their work was more subtle and more organic so that no part could be adequately appreciated save in its relation to the whole. What is true of the artists of the early sixteenth century is true, in a great measure, of their contemporary, Ariosto. His technique was similar to theirs, and consequently distinct from the fifteenth century technique of Boiardo. An examination of the structure of the first few cantos of the *Orlando Furioso* will suffice to prove that its apparently haphazard transitions have often a logical character, and that Charles James Fox was not convicting himself of literary incompetence when he described his favourite poem as being "the most regular and connected of epics."

The first stanza strikes with amazing precision the note that is to be sustained throughout.

> Le donne, i cavallier, l' arme, gli amori,
> Le cortesie, l' audaci imprese io canto,
> Che furo al tempo che passaro i Mori
> D' Africa il mare, e in Francia nocquer tanto,
> Seguendo l' ire e i giovenil furori
> D' Agramante lor re, che si diè vanto
> Di vendicar la morte di Troiano
> Sopra re Carlo imperator romano.

> Of Loves and Ladies, Knights and Arms I sing,
> Of Courtesies and many a Daring Feat;
> And from those ancient days my story bring,
> When Moors from Afric passed in hostile fleet,
> And ravaged France, with Agramant their king,
> Flushed with his youthful rage and furious heat;
> Who on King Charles, the Roman emperor's head
> Had vowed due vengeance for Troyano dead.

Orlando Furioso, I, 1.

Knights and ladies moved to gallant deeds by love and courtesy, the twin pillars of the moral world of romance, are the theme of Ariosto's song, and the obvious reminiscence of the first line of the *Aeneid* aptly suggests the classical spirit which is to pervade the whole. The poem is to be a romance and not an epic, for the fate of individuals rather than of empires is the centre of interest, but the setting is the historical realm of Charlemagne, with whatever fabulous additions, and not the dream-world of Bretagne. The *Orlando Innamorato* depicts a crisis in the fortunes of the Emperor which it leaves unsettled, and this is neither forgotten nor neglected in the sequel.

The second stanza emphasises the importance of Orlando, the titular hero, and the novelty of the rôle assigned to him, while the third passes to Ruggiero who, as the fabled progenitor of the House of Este, which it is Ariosto's purpose to glorify, becomes, in many ways, more truly the hero of the poem than Orlando himself. The threads of the story, as it had been left by Boiardo, are then gathered up; and in the tenth stanza Ariosto begins his own tale with the flight of Angelica from the field of battle into the neighbouring forest. Here she at once meets her unwelcome lover, Rinaldo. She flys in haste, and reaches the bank of a stream, near which stands the pagan Ferraù, who is searching for his lost helmet. He intervenes to protect Angelica from Rinaldo, and during their fight she gallops off. The contest, however, is brief and they unite to pursue her.

Ferrau soon finds himself once again by the bank
of the stream that he had left and resumes his interrupted search for his helmet. This helmet had formerly
belonged to Argalia, Angelica's brother, whose shade
now rises before Ferrau's astonished eyes, reminds
him of the promise recorded in the *Orlando Innamorato*, and suggests that he should seek to win a
helmet from Orlando or Rinaldo; to which Ferrau
agrees. All this has, at first sight, the air of an idle
digression, but it recalls the opening scenes of the
Orlando Innamorato, where Angelica appears in
hostile and treacherous guise, and thus prepares
the way for the substitution of Bradamante as the
true heroine of the poem. Ariosto can now drop
Ferrau, and go back to Rinaldo, but as the position
of the pursued is more exciting than that of the
pursuer, he passes quickly from him to Angelica,
merely taking occasion to indicate that Rinaldo's
famous horse Baiardo is independently following the
flying damsel. Her meeting with Sacripante serves to
reveal her character, and to give occasion for some
much admired descriptive stanzas, but its part in the
plot is to enable Sacripante to delay Rinaldo when he
again comes up with Angelica, who can thus escape
from both and continuing her flight alone meet with
further adventures.

Before this happens Bradamante has appeared on
the scene in the guise of an unknown knight who
overthrows Sacripante, and rides away without pause.

To readers of the *Orlando Innamorato*, however, Angelica was the better known and more interesting character, and Ariosto therefore follows her fortunes.

She encounters a hermit, who by magic arts persuades Rinaldo that Orlando has got possession of Angelica, and sends him towards Paris in hot pursuit. Of Orlando and Ruggiero we have as yet seen nothing and since both will be needed in connection with the fresh dangers to which Angelica is shortly to be exposed, she disappears from the story for the present. To whom shall Ariosto turn? The choice lies, in effect, between Rinaldo and Bradamante, Ferrau and Sacripante being only minor characters. He chooses Rinaldo, probably because his close relation to Angelica makes the transition less abrupt than by passing direct from one heroine to the other. The part which Rinaldo has, for the moment, to play being of little interest, we leave him as soon as he is fairly on the way to new adventures, and return to his sister. Bradamante is searching for her lover, Ruggiero, and meets by accident with one Pinabello, and, in course of relating his own misfortunes, he tells her that Ruggiero has fallen into the power of a magician who in the sequel proves to be Ruggiero's devoted guardian, Atlante. He possesses a flying horse and a magic shield whose brilliance stuns all beholders. Both shield and steed figure prominently in the subsequent course of the story. Pinabello, who is of the clan of Maganza, discovers Bradamante's identity and resolves, if possible, to kill her. He tricks her into falling into a cave, where she meets with the fay Melissa, who afterwards acts in some sort as her protecting angel, and learns the glorious fortunes of the progeny who are destined to be born to her and Ruggiero. These flattering histories of the House of Este, which recur at various points in the poem, are to us digressions, and tedious ones, but they were, of course, an essential part of Ariosto's plan, though their strictly aesthetic justification might prove difficult. Melissa tells Bradamante that to rescue Ruggiero she will need an enchanted ring, the same which formerly belonged to Angelica, and which like the horse and shield is indispensable to the development of the story. Bradamante frees Ruggiero, but at the moment of success he is, by the arts of Atlante, borne off on the flying horse. As Bradamante must now leave the stage Ariosto has again to choose which thread of his story he will take up. His choice again falls upon Rinaldo, both because we may be supposed to feel more interest in him than in Ruggiero, who, in the *Orlando Furioso*, has been little more than a name, and because his adventures offer more scope for variation of scene and interest.

Rinaldo has been sent to Scotland to get the help of which Charlemagne is in need after his defeat by the Saracens. On landing in Scotland he is told of an accusation of unchastity which has been brought against Ginevra, the daughter of the king. The story of Ginevra need not detain us, but we must notice that though it seems a mere detached episode it serves to introduce to us in a favourable light the family of the King of Scotland, and thus prepares us to take an interest in the fortunes of his son Zerbino whose love story is one of the most important and distinctly marked features of the *Orlando Furioso*.

Rinaldo's return is devoid of incident, so that we can now go back to Ruggiero. Whither has he been borne on the back of the flying horse? It is the purpose of the magician to separate him from Bradamante therefore he must be taken to some distant spot where he can be persuaded or compelled to remain. The choice of the island of Alcina is a rational one from this point of view, for the island is situated in the remotest eastern seas, and Alcina herself is a fay who can keep Ruggiero enthralled by her seductions. In this perfectly natural manner Ariosto constructs a link which is vital to his tale; for, as we have learnt from Boiardo, Astolfo is in Alcina's power. Ruggiero will meet him and enable him to escape from her toils, and Astolfo will thus be free to undertake the adventures and perform the feats upon which the fate of Charlemagne's Empire ultimately turns.

It cannot be necessary to carry this analysis further. We have seen enough to prove that the *Orlando Furioso* is no mere casual aggregate of brilliant scenes,

but that Ariosto shows great capacity for the logical
ordering of most complex material and justifies his
own repeated allusion to the "many threads which
he needs for his great canvas."

If in method Ariosto differs from Boiardo, in another essential matter he follows in his footsteps.
Romance may be predominantly of feeling or of
action, and each type has its own beauty. The
Orlando Innamorato belongs to the latter kind and
here Ariosto introduces no substantial change. Tem-
peramental bias combined with circumstances to
make this course practically inevitable. Ariosto was
absent-minded but he was not in truth dreamy. His
keen sense of reality and his vivid pictorial imagination were almost bound to result in a preference for
the definiteness of action over the vague intricacies
of sentiment. To him, as to the society in which he
lived, the objects that excited emotions were of more
compelling interest than those emotions themselves.
Nevertheless his insight into character was greater
than that of Boiardo, though his feeling for human
nature nowhere degenerates into the sentimentality
of Tasso.

The world of chivalry presented an abundant supply
of actions, but the task of selecting only those which
were compatible with the claims of beauty was by
no means an easy one. The path between too little
and too much was narrow and hard to find. It is
notorious that descriptions of heaven are commonly

tedious and unreal, and this seems to arise not so
much from lack of imagination on the part of their
authors, as from a nervous fear of including in the
picture of an ideal state trivial or unworthy elements,
with the frequent result that all life and vigour are
banished. The lover of beauty is exposed to a very
similar danger. His love of beauty will necessarily
make him critical. He will be inclined to put aside
first this and then that feature of existence until he
has so limited the scope of his appeal that it is no
longer capable of producing any strong impression,
and his work becomes finicking. The ideal is not a
transcript of the actual but every deviation from
reality extorts its price, for not the finest chemistry
of art can resolve the stuff of life so perfectly into its
elements as to lose no scrap of loveliness by the
banishment of a portion of fact. There was much
in the romances of chivalry that Ariosto's cultivated
taste must have tempted him to exclude, but to have
yielded freely to this temptation would have emascu-
lated his poem; as many will feel that Tennyson has
done in his *Idylls of the King*. His cool good sense
protected him against any such danger. As he had
refused to weaken his style by a pedantic purism of
language, so also he refused to weaken the substance
of his poem by rejecting without further parley all
those elements of the traditional romances that might
seem open to censure. It was the easier for him to
take this course by reason of the fact that his world,

though geographically narrow, was spiritually wide, hampered by few conventions, and abounding in vigour. The men and women for whom Ariosto wrote had tastes rather over-robust than prudish, delighted in movement and pageantry, and were ready to welcome vivid experience in almost any guise.

The opposite danger of the uncritical acceptance of some of the coarser and uglier features of human life was therefore the more insistent. In many cases civilisation was little more than a veneer. If there was much freshness and strength, there was much also of the brutality of the savage, and horrors, which delicate feeling would immediately have rejected, were often, as some of the contemporary Italian "novelle" prove, thought no more than pleasantly exciting. Nothing resembling the eighth canto of the *Orlando Innamorato* is to be found in the *Orlando Furioso*. No suggestion of brutality is ever elaborated, though perhaps some of these suggestions might have been better omitted, as, for instance, in the description of Orlando's treatment of the thieves from whom he had just rescued Isabella:

> Poi li strascina fuor de la spelonca,
> Dove facea grande ombra un vecchio sorbo.
> Orlando con la spada i rami tronca,
> E quelli attacca per vivanda al corbo.
> Non bisognò catena in capo adonca;
> Che per purgare il mondo di quel morbo,
> L' arbor medesmo gli uncini prestolli,
> Con che pel mento Orlando ivi attaccolli.

He after drags them bound without the cave,
Where an old service-tree its shadow throws.
Orlando lops the branches with his glaive,
And hangs the thieves, a banquet for the crows:
Nor chain and crook for such a deed did crave:
For ready hooks the tree itself bestows,
To purge the world; where by the chin uphung,
These, on the branches, bold Orlando strung.

Orlando Furioso, XIII, 41.

Even here the action would hardly attract attention if the actor had not been Orlando. Ariosto's good taste is, in general, so unfailing that a distinguished and by no means over-indulgent critic has said, "This Homer never nods." Yet one or two lapses may be discovered, which are worth notice for the light that they throw upon a highly-characteristic feature of Ariosto's mind.

The story of Isabella and Zerbino, their love, their separation, the death of Zerbino as a consequence of his duel with Mandricardo in defence of Orlando's arms and Isabella's desperate grief, has, perhaps, more of an ideal character than any other part of the *Orlando Furioso*. Isabella, though a Saracen, is persuaded by a hermit to abandon her intention of killing herself upon Zerbino's body, and to enter a nunnery. On the way thither she meets with Rodomonte, King of Sarza, the most terrible of the pagan champions. He falls passionately in love, and after disposing of the hermit, urges his suit with an ardour that approaches violence. In order to escape his

unwelcome admiration, and preserve inviolate her
faith to Zerbino, Isabella tells him that she knows of
a magic potion which confers invulnerability, and
which she will forthwith prepare for him, if he
promises to respect her honour in the meanwhile.
Rodomonte agrees, and Isabella, having compounded
the necessary materials, anoints herself, and induces
Rodomonte, who is a little under the influence of
wine, to test the efficacy of the potion by striking
her with his sword. The result Ariosto describes as
follows:

> Bagnossi, come disse, e lieta porse
> All' incauto Pagano il collo ignudo,
> Incauto, e vinto anco dal vino forse,
> Incontra a cui non vale elmo né scudo,
> Quell' uom bestial le prestò fede, e scórse
> Sí colla mano e sí col ferro crudo
> Che del bel capo, già d' Amore albergo,
> Fe' tronco rimanere il petto e il tergo.
>
> Quel fe' tre balzi, e funne udita chiara
> Voce ch' uscendo nominò Zerbino,
> Per cui seguire ella trovò si rara
> Via di fuggir di man del Saracino.
> Alma, ch' avesti più la fede cara
> E 'l nome, quasi ignoto e peregrino
> Al tempo nostro, de la castitade,
> Che la tua vita e la tua verde etade,
>
> Vattene in pace, alma beata e bella.
> Cosi i miei versi avezzon forza, come
> Ben m' affaticherei con tutta quella
> Arte che tanto il parlar orna e come,

Perchè mille e mill' anni e più, novella
Sentisse il mondo del tuo chiaro nome.
Vattene in pace alla superna sede,
E lascia all' altre esempio di tua fede.

All' atto incomparabile e stupendo,
Dal cielo il Creator giù gli occhi volse,
E disse: Più di quella ti commendo
La cui morte a Tarquinio il regno tolse;
E per questo una legge fare intendo
Tra quelle mie che mai tempo non sciolse,
La qual per le inviolabil acque giuro
Che non muterà secolo futuro.

She washed, as said, and gladly did decline
Her neck to that unthinking pagan's brand;
Unthinking, and perhaps o'ercome with wine,
Which neither helm, nor mail, nor shield withstand.
That brutish man believed her, and, in sign
Of faith, so struck with cruel steel and hand,
That her fair head, erewhile Love's place of rest,
He severed from the snowy neck and breast.

This made three bounds, and thence in accents clear
Was heard a voice which spake Zerbino's name,
To follow whom, escaping Sarza's peer,
So rare a way was taken by the dame.
Spirit! which nobly did esteem more dear
Thy plighted faith, and chaste and holy name,
(Things hardly known and foreign to our time,)
Than thine own life and thine own blooming prime!

Depart in peace, O spirit blest and fair!
—So had my verses power! as evermore
I would assay with all that happy care,
Which so adorns and points poetic lore!

And, as renowned should be thy story rare,
Thousands and thousands of long years and more!
—Depart in peace to radiant realms above,
And leave to earth the example of thy love!

His eyes from heaven did the Creator bend,
At the stupendous and unequalled feat,
And said: "I thee above that dame commend
Whose death drove Tarquin from his royal seat;
And I to register a law intend,
Mid those which ages change not as they fleet,
Which—I attest the inviolable river—
Unchanged through future times shall last for ever."

Orlando Furioso, XXIX, 25–28.

Pathetic beauty, just up to but not beyond the point where it becomes painful, is obviously Ariosto's design in this passage, but he has gravely injured the effect by four words: "Quel fe' tre balzi." The picture that they call up is at once shocking and absurd, utterly out of keeping with the context as a whole. How came Ariosto to write them? Something may be attributed to the deficient sense of the horrible which, as we have seen, belonged to the age. Ariosto is perhaps sinking for a moment to the level of his contemporaries. More probably, his fault was due to the excess of a virtue, namely the intensely pictorial and realistic character of his imagination which, enabling him to see with the utmost vividness every detail of his imaginary scenes, tempted him to describe them exactly as they happened.

Another instance of defective taste may be noticed

in the thirty-sixth canto. The two warlike heroines, Bradamante and Marfisa, have engaged in conflict, and Marfisa has been repeatedly overthrown by the touch of Bradamante's magic lance. They continue the struggle on foot, dropping their swords and drawing their daggers. At this point, Ruggiero, who has been looking on, interferes, takes away their daggers and begs them to desist, but in vain for they attack each other:

> A pugni e a calci, poi ch' altro non hanno.

> Each other they with fists and feet attack.
>
> *Orlando Furioso*, XXXVI, 50.

Ariosto can scarcely have intended to make Bradamante and Marfisa appear ridiculous. Both are described as being in strength and skill, as well as in all knightly virtues, equal to the bravest of the Paladins. It should have been physically impossible for even Ruggiero to deprive them of their weapons, and morally impossible for two such heroines to descend to the undignified expedient of blows and kicks. Ariosto, once again misled by his realistic imagination, has for the moment become oblivious of the difference between his heroines and the women of real life, and has represented female recourse to violence as having here the vulgar ineffectiveness that belongs to it in the world of reality.

If these two incidents have been treated at somewhat disproportionate length, the fault may perhaps be excused by the consideration that matters in them-selves small may do much to illuminate character.

Since Ariosto conceived of his poem as a whole which was to be everywhere beautiful, he could not fail to observe the contrast that it presented both to the traditional world of chivalry and to the world of fact. The first of these contrasts was by far the less profound, and for that very reason is the more con-spicuous; for here something could be achieved by modifications of detail, while the real world was, broadly speaking, too alien to figure prominently in Ariosto's scheme. In the world of chivalry there was much that was beautiful, and its ideals, in the main, were Ariosto's own. If it had been otherwise, the *Orlando Furioso* must have become a burlesque, and this, in spite of Ariosto's frequent use of irony, it certainly is not. Love and friendship were the dominant emotions, courage, courtesy and honour the chief virtues of a knight of romance. With regard to the importance of love Ariosto is at one with the romantic tradition. For him sexual love is beautiful, and he is nowhere ashamed of its mani-festations, though he sometimes hints that it is, after all, a madness at war with common sense. Physical chastity is no part of his ideal, for even in the case of Isabella it is her loyalty to Zerbino, and her readiness to sacrifice life itself rather than yield lovelessly, which arouses his admiration. Many who would nominally accept the view that love is beautiful yet feel for the details of sex a repulsion which is fundamentally aesthetic. Ariosto does not share this feeling and therefore has no motive for excluding such details from his picture. He accepts, perhaps more logically than tradition, the consequences of chivalric principles. He is, of course, not blind to the unaesthetic brutality of one-sided and selfish desire, and only in one instance, that of Angelica and the hermit, lapses into depicting it.

With regard to his general attitude towards women the contrast with earlier ages is more plain. Women may be of a clinging or of a self-dependent type, and either may have aesthetic value, but Ariosto's preference was for the latter kind, though he introduces the former in greater numbers. He shared the widespread contemporary opinion that their natural capacities were little if at all inferior to those of men, and frequently expresses his belief that in sexual and other matters they should be treated as on an equality with them.

Of friendship he makes less than Boiardo, but he is not indifferent to it, and quite appreciates the beauty of the affection between Orlando and Brandimarte, and of Zerbino's adoring gratitude for the inestimable services of the former.

Courage belongs of right to all heroes of romance. Of the courtesy which repays every debt with a service of equal or greater magnitude Ariosto gives, without irony, an extravagant example in the relations of Ruggiero and Leone. His conception of honour includes not only the strictest fair play, but a meticulous regard for truth. He, in effect, apologises for Bradamante's deception of Brunello, and makes Rinaldo, in the case of Ginevra, guard himself against even unintentional falsehood.

Having so much in common with the ideals of chivalry Ariosto could accept many of its typical incidents almost without change, but nevertheless certain modifications had to be made in the interests of his own view of beauty. If the scenes of romance had all been joyful they would have become monotonous. Many were pathetic, and Ariosto could not venture to exclude pathos without fatally narrowing his emotional range. How was he to include it and yet avoid such a degree of tension as would have injured the harmonious colouring of his picture? He has no single answer to this problem, but adapts his method to the circumstances, seeking in each case to prevent the sympathy aroused from becoming excessive by the use of a remarkable variety of devices, sometimes extraneous to, sometimes within the field of the episode in question. Olympia's heart-broken lament over Bireno's desertion is highly pathetic, and in the despairing loneliness of her abandonment there seems to be no ray of light, but Ariosto deliberately lowers its effect by an abrupt and matter-of-fact transition to another topic, as if to remind us that it is, after all, but a story and need not give us any serious pain. More often some feature of comfort belonging to the actual situation is brought in to serve the same purpose. When Zerbino is failing under the blows of Mandricardo, Fiordiligi's thought that once Brandimarte or Orlando know what has happened the Tartar will not long enjoy his triumph is clearly designed to relieve the painfulness of Zerbino's defeat. Isabella's grief and death are both softened. The one by the introduction of the slightly platitudinous old hermit, and the absurd extravagance of his end, and the other by a peculiar harmony and sweetness of language, by Rodomonte's sincere and lasting regret for his action and, more than all, by the fact that our final thoughts of Isabella are not associated with suffering but with her blissful reunion with Zerbino.

> Dio così disse, e fe' serena intorno
> L' aria, e tranquillo il mar più che mai fusse,
> Fe' l' alma casta al terzo ciel ritorno,
> E in braccio al suo Zerbin si ricondusse.

> So spake the Sire; and cleared the ambient air,
> And hushed beyond its wont the heaving main,
> To the third heaven her chaste soul made repair,
> And in Zerbino's arms was locked again.

Orlando Furioso, XXIX, 30.

Orlando's outburst of grief at the funeral of Brandimarte likewise contains many features which tend to diminish our sorrow; features in this instance arising directly from the situation. It may be noticed in passing that the classical allusions which to us are so frigid, were quite natural and sincere to the men of Ariosto's day, and must not be held to detract from the merit of what is perhaps the most faultless expression of deep feeling to be found in the whole of the *Orlando Furioso*.

It is doubtless for similar reasons that Ariosto dismisses his villains, such as Bireno, Odorico and Gabrina, with contemptuous haste from the scene when they have played their parts.

Pathos was not the only element of the romances of chivalry that needed modification, and the delicate irony which runs through Ariosto's poem has here one of its chief sources. It is Ariosto's method of dealing with traditional motives that he must retain yet could not, on aesthetic grounds, whole-heartedly accept. Religious zeal is a dominant impulse in the Carolingian epics. In the courtly society of Ferrara at the dawn of the sixteenth century it would have been an anachronism, and any attempt to use it seriously as an aesthetic principle must have failed. If, as some have supposed, there is a tendency in the *Orlando Furioso* to present pagan heroes and heroines in an unfavourable light it is not very well marked. Isabella is a pagan, Brandimarte was originally a pagan, and Ruggiero himself and his sister Marfisa are pagans almost throughout the poem. The zeal of the hermit for the conversion of Isabella is treated with a certain irony, and it is not even quite plain that he was successful.

Supernatural characters are handled with still less seriousness. The Spirit of Discord dwells in a monastery. She has neglected the task which the Archangel Michael has given her, of stirring up strife among the pagans, and he goes to remind her of it:

> Al monister, dove altre volte avea
> La Discordia veduta, drizzò l' ali.
> Trovolla ch' in capitolo sedea
> A nuova elezïon degli ufficiali;
> E di veder diletto si prendea
> Volar per capo a' frati i brevïali.
> Le man le pose l' Angelo nel crine
> E pugna e calci le diè senza fine.
>
> Again he to that monastery flew,
> Where whilom he had Discord seen; and there
> Seated in chapter sees her, while anew
> Their yearly officers elected are,
> She taking huge delight these friers to view,
> That at each other hurled their books of prayer.
> His hand within her locks the archangel twists,
> And deals her endless scathe with feet and fists.
>
> *Orlando Furioso*, XXVII, 37.

That the hare-brained Astolfo should become the favourite of the gods, should ascend to the Earthly Paradise, should receive from S. John a good dinner, at which the apples proved particularly fine, and should go with him to the Kingdom of the Moon in order to recover from the Valley of Lost Things the brains of Orlando; and finally should, by miracles of the utmost extravagance, save the Empire of

Charlemagne, and bring Agramante to ruin, approaches more nearly to sustained burlesque than anything else in the poem.

To the primitive mind war is the noblest occupation of man, and physical prowess his best title to fame. This point of view is reflected in traditional romance. The Paladins, and in particular Orlando, are persons of superhuman strength whose customary employment is the slaughter of hosts of pagans.

Ariosto could not, of course, banish fighting from his tale, and there is no reason to think that he would have wished to do so if it had been possible. He doubtless admired courage, and in that age more than others every form of vigorous enterprise touched a responsive chord in men's hearts. He was, however, much too intellectual to reckon physical strength among the greatest of human gifts; and all Italy knew what war was really like. If he could not leave out these things, he could, at any rate, modify the effect that they produced upon the reader. Orlando was, traditionally, the strongest of the Paladins, and the slayer of innumerable heathen. Ariosto allows him to retain both characteristics, but exaggerates them until they become ridiculous, and emphasises his ironical intention by mock appeals to the authority of Archbishop Turpin. In the same manner the duel between Zerbino and Marfisa is a parody of chivalric ideas. They fight like true knights for the possession of a lady, the hag Gabrina, but it

is the loser who is to get her. Zerbino, ignorant
at the time of his opponent's sex, proves unequal to
the contest, and goes down before a female lance.
Ariosto's smiles are not reserved for chivalry. In his
adventurous journey to the infernal regions Astolfo
meets Lidia, who is an obvious counterpart of
Francesca da Rimini, and whose narrative of the
causes of her punishment is an ironical commentary
on Dante's moral outlook. That men who have been
ungrateful for the gift of love are consigned to a
deeper hell, where Astolfo does not penetrate, reveals
that Ariosto condemned in all seriousness the cruelties
of sex. A circumstance not, perhaps, very germane to
an appreciation of the *Orlando Furioso*, but interesting
in relation to the character of its author. Nor is irony
directed against the world of his own day absent, as
in the mocking couplet that closes the account of the
objects to be found in the Valley of Lost Things:

> Sol la pazzia non v' è poca né assai
> Che sta qua giù, né se ne parte mai.

> Save only madness seen not here at all
> Which dwells below nor leaves this earthly ball.

Orlando Furioso, XXXIV, 81.

And not infrequently in the exordia to the cantos.

We have seen how Boiardo turned this customary
break in the narrative to poetic account. Ariosto
makes a more regular and fuller use of the same
opportunity. His exordia become distinct features of
his poem, and good judges have reckoned them among

E O   10

its greatest beauties. They are of a varied character,
but general reflections on the ways of man and
woman predominate, and most have a slightly
satirical flavour, as for example:

> Ben furo avventurosi i cavallieri
> Ch' erano a quella età, che nei valloni,
> Ne le scure spelonche e boschi fieri,
> Tane di serpi, d' orsi e di leoni,
> Trovavan quel che nei palazzi altieri
> A pena or trovar puon giudici buoni;
> Donne, che ne la lor più fresca etade
> Sien degne d' aver titol di beltade.

> Those ancient cavaliers right happy were,
> Born in an age, when in the gloomy wood,
> In valley, and in cave wherein the bear,
> Serpent, and lion, hid their savage brood,
> They could find that, which now in palace rare
> Is hardly found by judges proved and good;
> Women, to wit, who in their freshest days
> Of beauty worthily deserve the praise.
>
> *Orlando Furioso*, XIII, 1.

When he is ironical Ariosto is always good-humoured,
but with reference to his contemporaries he occasionally allows himself so far to depart from the general
tone of his poem as to give vent to feelings of genuine
indignation. Sometimes implicitly, as in the description of the sack of Biserta in the fortieth canto, but
more often without any veil, as in his comparison
of the soldiery who were devastating Italy to the
Harpies, or in his exhortation to the Christian powers

to remember their faith and turn their arms against
"the unclean Turk" with its bitter

> O d' ogni vizio fetida sentina,
> Dormi, Italia imbrïaca,

O Italy of every vice the fetid sewer you drunken sleep.

Orlando Furioso, XVII, 76.

Aesthetically connected with this mood is the epic
character which, though quite subordinate to romance,
belongs to parts of the *Orlando Furioso*. Rodomonte
raging through the streets of Paris, and retreating
like a baffled lion before the vast crowd of his
enemies who cannot press home their advantage
against his single might, is an epic figure. Hardly
less epic is the final duel of the three champions of
Christendom against Agramante, Gradasso and Sobrino, which reaches a fitting climax when the fall
of his friend Brandimarte inspires Orlando with such
titanic fury that even Gradasso turns pale with fear,
and both he and Agramante sink helplessly under the
Paladin's strokes.

Ariosto's feeling for natural beauty may be briefly
dealt with. Not because it is a factor of small importance, it is far from being that, but because in this
respect he differs scarcely at all from his predecessor,
save in his greater command of language suited to
express his conceptions. What has been said of
Boiardo's preference for joyous and humane land-
scapes applies equally to Ariosto; and of his power of
depicting them we have already had one example in

the stanza quoted in illustration of his style. The *Orlando Furioso*, like other romances, is mainly concerned with the adventures of individual knights and ladies; and it has even been thought that the, at least apparently, haphazard nature of their proceedings is symbolic of the uncontrolled spirit of the Renaissance. In a poem so full of action the characters are many; yet it is in characterisation that its greatest weakness has often been supposed to lie. The charge is perhaps not entirely without foundation, however much it may have been exaggerated. If the *Orlando Furioso* is compared with the masterpieces of the drama or the best psychological novels its deficiencies are patent. But the test is hardly a fair one. Ariosto's poem is a poem of adventure, and a poem in which everything must contribute to the general effect of harmonious beauty. These conditions necessarily imposed limits on the extent to which it could be made a vehicle for the delineation of the finer shades of character. The rapidity of movement which distinguishes it would alone have made impossible the elaboration of the subtle play of motive and feeling. It must be measured against works of its own kind, though there are perhaps none to be found which in this sphere so narrowly restrict the author's freedom. The romantic novels of Scott and of Dumas naturally suggest themselves, and the *Orlando Furioso* does not suffer much by the comparison; indeed in regard to depicting female character Ariosto may claim the superiority. All his characters, both male and female, are, at any rate, distinct individuals who could not be confused with one another, and who, unlike the figures of Boiardo, remain consistent with themselves throughout the story. This alone is enough to show that the essentials of characterisation are present. Not infrequently there is something more and none of the chief persons of his tale can fairly be said to be quite devoid of interest. Many, of course, are borrowed from tradition, and are identical in name with characters in the *Orlando Innamorato*. In these cases Ariosto is not bound by the conceptions of his predecessor. The Orlando of the *Furioso* is very different from the Orlando of the *Innamorato*, and Astolfo, Bradamante, Angelica and others undergo more or less conspicuous changes.

In the main Orlando is treated with more seriousness and intensity than any other figure in the poem. He is not a model of knightly perfection, but we are made to feel that he is a great man who, with all his errors, never loses, so long as reason remains to him, his nobility of soul. His love for Angelica is an overwhelming passion. His bitter lament for what he regards as his weakness in allowing Charlemagne to take her from him gives at once the key to his disposition. It is too long for complete quotation but the following stanzas will give some idea of its effect:

> Di questo Orlando avea gran doglia, e seco
> Indarno a sua sciocchezza ripensava.

Cor mio (dicea), come vilmente teco
Mi son portato! oimè, quanto mi grava
Che potendoti aver notte e dì meco,
Quando la tua bontà non mel negava,
T' abbia lasciato in man di Namo porre,
Per non sapermi a tanta injuria opporre!

Non aveva ragione io di scusarme?
E Carlo non m' avria forse disdetto:
Se pur disdetto, e chi potea sforzarme?
Chi ti mi volea torre al mio dispetto?
Non poteva io venir più tosto all' arme?
Lasciar più tosto trarmi il cor del petto?
Ma né Carlo né tutta la sua gente
Di tormiti per forza era possente.

Almen l' avesse posta in guardia buona
Dentro a Parigi o in qualche rocca forte.
Che l' abbia data a Namo mi consona,
Sol perchè a perder l' abbia a questa sorte.
Chi la dovea guardar meglio persona
Di me? ch' io dovea farlo fino a morte:
Guardala più ch 'l cor, che gli occhi miei;
E dovea e potea farlo, e pur nol fei.

This in Orlando moved great grief, and he
Lay thinking on his folly pass't in vain.
"My heart," he said, "oh! how unworthily
I bore myself! and, out! alas what pain,
(When night and day I might have dwelt with thee
Since this thou didst not in thy grace disdain)
To have let them place thee in old Namus hand!
Witless a wrong so crying to withstand.

Might I not have excused myself? The king
Had not perchance gainsaid my better right—

Or if he had gainsaid my reasoning,
Who would have taken thee in my despite?
Why not have armed, and rather let them wring
My heart out of my breast? But not the might
Of Charles and all his host, had they been tried,
Could have availed to tear thee from my side.

Oh had he placed her but in strong repair,
Guarded in some good fort or Paris town!
—Since he would trust her to Duke Namo's care,
That he should lose her in this way alone
Sorts with my wish. Who would have kept the fair
Like me, that would for her to death have gone?
Have kept her better than my heart or sight:
Who should and could, yet did not what I might."

                                  Orlando Furioso, VIII, 73–76.

The dream which follows is also most vividly
imagined. In contrast to Ruggiero under similar
circumstances, Orlando is perfectly indifferent to the
charms that Olympia displays when he rescues her
from the Orca, and is unfeignedly glad when honour
permits him to entrust the duty of protecting her
and avenging her wrongs to the King of Ireland.
The cumulative effect of discovering proof more and
more indisputable that Angelica belongs in heart and
person to Medoro and is lost to him for ever destroys
his mental balance. The gradual onset of madness is
described with great force and considerable psychological insight, and it is no mere accident that
these scenes are literally the centre of the poem.
By Italians they have even been compared to the

insanity of Lear. But the comparison is inapt. Orlando's loss of reason is far from being pure tragedy for the exaggeration of his physical strength at other times compels Ariosto to attribute to him feats still more impossible in the rage of madness. This was unavoidable, but Ariosto may not have regretted the necessity. It enabled him to remain true to his general principle of keeping the stress of even his most highly-wrought scenes below the point at which the emotional equilibrium is destroyed. That Orlando should at last meet Angelica, unrecognising and unrecognised, and should pursue her with bestial fury, is a fit ending to the tale of his unhappy love. Loyalty and friendship though not honour have to yield to his passion. He is of few words—is it possible that he is the original of the strong silent man?—but he vows to fight against the islanders of Ebuda before the damsel has finished speaking. He will save Olympia, he will rescue and protect Isabella and earn the devotion of Zerbino, but he has no care for the plight in which he leaves the Emperor, and even Brandimarte must not know of his search for Angelica.

The impression of intensity and power is heightened by several delicate touches. Orlando sets out from Paris by night and in disguise. He comes to the gate and whispers to the captain of the guard, "io sono il Conte." No more is needed. At once the gate is opened and the drawbridge lowered. For the soldiers of Charlemagne, and indeed for all Christendom,

there is only one "Conte," and he must be obeyed
without question. When naked and insane he rushes
upon the Christian camp before Biserta all the Paladins, even the careless and light-hearted Astolfo, are
moved to tears by the spectacle of his degradation.

Rinaldo and Orlando are both Paladins and both in
love with the same maiden, yet they are quite distinct.
In some respects they may be compared to Athos
and d'Artagnan, though Orlando is more truly noble
than the self-conscious Comte de la Fère. Rinaldo,
if not equal to d'Artagnan, is, in his combination of
impetuous gallantry and kindness of heart with a
slightly cynical good sense, at least reminiscent of
Dumas' famous hero. In illustration may be mentioned his attitude towards Ginevra, his refusal to
drink of the magic cup which tests the fidelity of
wives and the reasons that he gives for it; and his
speech to Ferrau:

> Quanto fia meglio, amandola tu ancora,
> Che tu le venga a traversar la strada,
> A ritenerla e farle far dimora,
> Prima che più lontana se ne vada!
> Come l'avremo in potestate, allora
> Di chi esser de' si provi con la spada.
> Non so altrimente, dopo un lungo affanno,
> Che possa riuscirci altro che danno.

> "Then how much better, since our stake's the same,
> Thou, loving like myself shouldst mount and stay
> To wait this battle's end, the lovely dame,
> Before she fly yet further on her way.

> The lady taken we repeat our claim
> With naked faulchion to that peerless prey:
> Else by long toil I see not what we gain
> But simple loss and unrequited pain."
>
> *Orlando Furioso*, I, 20.

More than others Rinaldo is the same person in the *Orlando Innamorato* and in the *Furioso*. Nowhere is he more truly d'Artagnan than in explaining why he may take the golden chair from the garden of Morgana, though Orlando has thought it beneath his dignity to do so.

Ruggiero has some of the common defects of the hero of romance. He is handsome, brave, chivalrous and invincible—he could scarcely be otherwise—but of individual traits there are few. In his behaviour to Angelica he is, at any rate, not open to the charge of conventionality. His purpose is that of the hermit to whom reference has been made, and the incident may seem rather to imply an unchivalrous violence which, in him, would have been aesthetically fatal. But Ruggiero is young and in physique a model of knightly excellence. He can well be supposed to have acted without thinking too precisely upon the event, and to have shared the views which Sacripante expresses, on a not quite dissimilar occasion, with reference to the same lady. At the very moment when he must either change his course or descend to the level of Odorico and the hermit, Angelica becomes invisible.

Later he hurls his magic shield into a bottomless well because through it he has quite accidentally gained an advantage that may seem unfair over some knights with whom he has been jousting. The contrast most aptly illustrates the character of Ruggiero and the inconsistencies of customary honour, but neither here nor elsewhere is Ariosto directly concerned with morals. However natural Ruggiero's conduct both to Alcina and to Angelica may be, it has the unfortunate effect of giving the impression that his love for Bradamante is rather languid, an impression that is confirmed by many details, and which Ariosto never succeeds in removing. Other heroes can be more briefly noticed. Rodomonte is a figure of massive pride and ferocity, but hardly a character. Sacripante, the king who "makes tepid fountains of his eyes" (*O.F.* 1, 48), appears with effect in only one scene, but there he is skilfully drawn. The savage Mandricardo, Ferrau, Agramante and the cautious Sobrino are too slight for particular notice. There is a touch of pathos about the unrequited devotion of Atlante to his ward which makes him, magician though he is, almost human. Astolfo plays a most prominent part, but his character is not of commensurate interest. He is a rather paler copy of the Astolfo of the *Innamorato*, and has lost some of his humour, perhaps through becoming a favourite of the gods.

Ariosto is at his best in female characters of whom

the chief are Angelica, Marfisa and Bradamante, though some of the less conspicuous, such as Doralice, are of at least equal truth.

Unlike the other two heroines Angelica is purely feminine. Her weapon is beauty and she makes remorseless use of it for her own ends. From her woodland bower she emerges, "like Diana on the stage" (*O.F.* 1, 52), to her lover, Sacripante, excites his ardour by her caresses, while herself remaining perfectly cold, repudiates with scorn his, in truth not unnatural, suspicions of her conduct with regard to Orlando, graciously forgives him, and resolves to take advantage of his devotion exactly so long as may be convenient to her; self-centred vanity blinding her to the risks of this procedure. When considering, at a later date, whether she shall ask Orlando or Sacripante to accompany her back to the East, she is completely careless of the result for either of them and thinks only of the question which she will be able most easily to discard when she has done with him. Yet in the *Furioso* she is not, even before her meeting with Medoro, altogether so heartless as in the *Innamorato*. She steals Orlando's helmet chiefly in the hope of thus putting an end to the fight between him and Ferrau, and is genuinely distressed when it afterwards falls into the hands of the latter. She is proud and luxurious. She remembers with regretful longing the splendid palaces of her father, and preserves Orlando's ring, not out of any regard for the donor,

but simply because of its intrinsic value. Danger is
not to her taste. To be alone at nightfall by the
stormy sea without aid or shelter almost breaks her
spirit. Medoro, helpless and seemingly at the point
of death, arouses her pity, and, in tending him, pity
becomes love. He is only a humble soldier but for
him pride and beauty are forgotten. She yields un-
stintedly to their mutual passion, and returning with
him to her distant eastern home, passes from the
scene.

Marfisa stands at the opposite pole to Angelica. As
strong and skilled in arms as the bravest Paladin,
she is the incarnation of proud self-confidence, and
prefers like a true knight-errant to seek adventures
alone. She is young and beautiful but, save her
beauty, has nothing conspicuously feminine about her.
Love has not the slightest place in her mind. Her
male companions are companions and nothing more,
though she frankly admires Ruggiero's strength and
courage. She is endowed with humour and is a
courteous and affectionate friend and, as she proves
in the case of Brunello, a not implacable enemy; but
she is impulsive, quick to anger and reckless of consequences to herself and others. With all this she is
not inhuman but rather the idealisation of a familiar
type. The schoolgirl who wishes to join in every
boyish sport, whose dream it is to excel all her companions in feats of strength, skill and courage, who
despises sentiment, is not an imaginary figure. Place

such a girl in the environment of the *Orlando Furioso*, make her companions men instead of boys, give her beauty and the power to realise her dreams of pre-eminence to their fullest extent, and you have Marfisa. Bradamante is also a warlike heroine, but she is not simply Marfisa in love, in spite of the fact that they have pride, strength, beauty and high spirit in common. She is more of a woman. Much less truly independent, less impulsive, less quick-tempered and less frank. She is proudly generous, disdaining, contrary to the advice of Melissa, to slay either Brunello or Atlante when she has them in her power. Love dominates her thoughts and actions. It leads her to neglect her duty to the Emperor; and jealousy, natural, though unfounded, is the cause of her over-whelming rage against Marfisa. The effect of her warlike prowess is greatly, and it is to be presumed, intentionally diminished by her possession of the magic lance which in any hands will unseat the strongest opponent. Sacripante and the cowardly Pinabello alone fall victims to her skill when deprived of its aid, and victory over the former is due rather to her steed than to herself. In her final duel with Ruggiero she is helpless. On more than one occasion Ariosto appears to determine her actions by regard for her high destiny as the ancestress of Cardinal Ippolito rather than from consideration of her character and circumstances as, for example, in the question of her marriage to Ruggiero. It is

possible, however, that this is no more than a piece
of superfluous realism.   Current convention de-
manded that all well brought-up young ladies should
submit implicitly to the judgment of their parents in
this matter, and Ariosto may, for the moment, have
forgotten that in a world where Bradamantes and
Marfisas existed such a convention would have been
absurd.

Of Ariosto's other feminine characters Doralice is
perhaps the best.   She is scarcely one of the leading
figures, but the scene in which she tries to persuade
Mandricardo to abandon the duel with Ruggiero is
more life-like than anything assigned to Bradamante,
and there are several other touches of nature.   Many
more such as Olympia, Isabella, Fiordespina, Fiordiligi and Gabrina are far from being mere puppets, but
it would be tedious to attempt to treat of them here.

The impression made upon our minds by the
Orlando Furioso is likely to undergo considerable
change with better acquaintance.   As soon as we
begin to read it we cannot fail to perceive that
Ariosto is bringing before us a series of constantly
varying pictures, that each of these pictures is perfectly clear and distinct, and that no one of them
occupies our attention for any great length of time.
We see a beautiful maiden flying wildly through the
forest, two knights meeting in deadly conflict, or
perhaps again in friendship, a great battle with some
renowned hero carrying death and destruction into

the serried ranks of the foe, an assault on a besieged city with blazing houses and terror-stricken crowds. The scene changes, and we gaze upon some limpid stream and listen to its gentle murmur while knights and maidens are meeting in love and joy or parting with grief and tears. Impregnable castles, baleful enchanters, mighty giants, gorgeous cities flaming with colour under the rays of an eastern sun pass before our eyes, only to be outshone by the super-human splendours of the Earthly Paradise and the strange wonders of the Circle of the Moon. The charm of youth, love and the fair beauty of nature is everywhere to be felt. No single emotion lasts long or reaches a painful height. The shining pictures flow by in endless succession, and we are perhaps inclined to think that all this is very pleasant, very brilliant, but hardly to be ranked as great poetry. Then perhaps we see deeper. We come to realise the unity of spirit and the subtle truth to nature that pervade these apparently fantastic scenes and, at length, we perceive that this is no mere series of attractive pictures that Ariosto has created, but that he has brought us almost unawares into an ideal world of the purest beauty and romance, yet marvellously complete and self-sufficing, and with all the air of reality and life, a world of fancy, most distinct but not divorced from fact, a world which cannot be described by any of the common antitheses, for it is neither Christian nor Pagan,

mediaeval nor modern, and which was not even the
common property of Italians during any period of
their Renaissance, however short. One or two of
Ariosto's contemporaries had feelings and ideals
similar to his and being endowed with like genius
were able to produce, in the medium of their own
arts, analogous creations. Such a one was Giorgione.
His incomparable *Sleeping Venus* is like no single
scene in the *Orlando Furioso*. Perhaps none of
Ariosto's heroines would have been quite worthy to
represent that vision of ideal loveliness. Yet if we
sought a visible symbol of the *Orlando Furioso*, an
expression not of its whole effect but of the essential
and individual quality of its romance, we should find
it here. So almost might Marfisa have slept, un-
troubled and unafraid. To some the comparison may
appear strained and Marfisa or Bradamante, those
"due belle e generose parde" (two fair and generous
pards—*Orlando Furioso*, xxxix, 69), too fiercely passionate to be likened to the tranquil beauty of
Giorgione's goddess in her divine repose. But grace
and loveliness are not inconsistent with possibilities
of energy or even of violence. The air of youthful
freshness and elasticity in this very figure, the feeling
that the repose of sleep could be exchanged on an
instant for the most vigorous action, has been observed by a distinguished art critic. A glance at the
Salome, which, whether Giorgione's own work or
not, is certainly in his spirit, ought to convince us that

the passion of heroines of the Renaissance was not
conceived as expressing itself in strained poses or
distorted features but was consistent with the most
complete outward calm. But this is not all. The
Orlando Furioso is a poem of incessant action but to
its heroes nothing is difficult, it is the secret of their
nature that to them the "boldest enterprises" should
be as effortless as sleep.

If we take into account the rest of Giorgione's art,
such as the Pitti *Concerto*, not to speak of other
works that have been very plausibly attributed to
him, we can see that he also was a realist, and a
realist of much the same fashion as Ariosto, who
never allowed his realism to lead him into a dis-
regard of the claims of beauty. Giorgione died young;
but if he had not it may well be that the irony of the
Furioso would have found its analogue in his work;
for it is improbable that a painter with so keen a
consciousness of both the ideal and the real should
never have noticed and wished to embody the contrast between them.

Whatever may have been the case with Giorgione,
Ariosto was fully aware of the depth of this contrast.
It scarcely admits of doubt that he created the world
of his poem, in part at least, as a refuge from a reality
that he despised. Such (he might have said) is the
world that I have fancied. In my world wounds do
not hurt, death is not bitter, grief is not ugly, beauty
reigns supreme. The real world is different; let us

bear with it as we may. The priests tell us of another life beyond the grave; and there, perchance, the gap between the realm of fancy and of fact is less wide. They babble drearily of an existence where Venus has no place, where there are no visions of fair women, glorious in black and gold, gazing down with love-lit eyes. It need not be as they say. Who knows? A smile plays about his lips, ironical, kind, indulgent. It is the soul of Ariosto.

Conclusion

To complete the picture something may be said about the fortunes of the *Orlando Furioso* in England. A number of our greatest writers have been acquainted with it, and a few have been largely indebted to it. Among the latter the most conspicuous is Spenser. His debt is patent and avowed, for it was his aim to surpass the *Orlando Furioso* in its own style. To enlarge upon this theme would, however, be to do over again work which Professor Courthope and Mr Dodge have executed in a manner which leaves little or nothing for their successors to add.

No later author is under obligations to the *Orlando Furioso* which can in extent and interest be compared with those of Spenser, but a few notices, which have not the very slightest pretension to be exhaustive, may collect for the reader's convenience information that would otherwise have to be sought in various quarters, and may suffice to indicate the curious fluctuations in popularity which Ariosto's master-piece has experienced; a subject which perhaps deserves more study than it has yet received.

In 1591 Sir John Harrington published the first English translation of the *Orlando Furioso*. He began with the twenty-eighth canto, and it is said that he only completed his work out of deference to the orders of Queen Elizabeth, who imposed it on him as a sort of penance for the interest that he had shown in the adventures of Giocondo and his partner. In the following year, and probably in consequence of Harrington's translation, Green produced a play of the same title as Ariosto's poem and containing many of the same names and incidents, though he has not scrupled to alter important features, such for example as Angelica's relations with Orlando, to suit his own purpose. The resemblance of the plot of *Much Ado about Nothing* and the Story of Ginevra has often been noted, but there is no reason to think that Shakespeare in fact owed anything to it, since one of the "novelle" of Bandello affords a far closer parallel.

Milton, of course, knew both the *Furioso* and the *Innamorato*, the latter presumably in Berni's version. His reference in *Paradise Regained* to Agrican's host before Albracca is familiar[1]. In *Paradise Lost* he owes something to Astolfo's journey to the moon, and one at least of his lines is a direct translation from a different part of the poem, though it cannot be said to have much significance[2]. An avowed translation is too characteristic of his tastes to be omitted.

> Then passed he to a flowery mountain green,
> Which once smelt sweet, now stinks so odiously:
> This was that gift (if you the truth will have)
> That Constantine to good Sylvester gave.
>
> *Orlando Furioso*, XXXIV, 80.
>
> *Of Reformation touching Church of England discipline.*

[1] *P.R.* III, 337–344.   [2] *O.F.* I, 2, line 2. *P.L.* line 16.

Nor was his knowledge unique. G. Hakewill's high estimate of Ariosto in his *Apology or Declaration of the Power and Providence of God*, where he ranks with the chief of the ancients, shows that even authors of little note admired the *Orlando Furioso*, but its greatest and most widespread popularity belongs to a considerably later date. From the first the men of the eighteenth century seem to have discovered something congenial in its spirit. Pope made use of it; Johnson, needless to say, had read it; and in 1731 Rolli found it worth while to publish an edition in London, a fact which testifies to a fairly large English demand for the poem. Charles Fox early fell in love with it and remained faithful all his life. His immense influence as a leader of fashion, a political chief and an acknowledged judge of good literature doubtless contributed powerfully to increase its vogue. Even John Wesley is said occasionally to have carried a copy about with him on his preaching tours, little as some parts of the poem might be supposed to meet his views; and so homely and British a poet as Crabbe can at least refer to Ariosto, though not in a way which necessarily implies any close knowledge of his works. A second translation had been published in 1757 which seems to have been a failure, most deservedly to judge from the specimen quoted by Professor Nicholson, but thirty years later Hoole's "transmutation of Ariosto's gold into lead" achieved remarkable success, and went through many editions in the course of the next few decades. Sir Walter Scott is known to have read the *Orlando Furioso* at frequent intervals for many years, and, in youth at any rate, to have thought it superior to Homer. In view of this fact it is perhaps surprising that his own romances owe so little to it, whether in their general spirit or in details. None of his characters are at all like any in the *Furioso*, unless the "Black Knight" may be supposed by reason of his physical qualities and his black armour to resemble Orlando.

Byron's obligations were greater and were not limited to the form of his verse, though they are otherwise hard to assess with precision. If he owed some of the lightness of touch which marks his poetry, and in particular *Don Juan*, to Ariosto, he was his debtor for much more than a few plagiarisms, and, nevertheless, in a manner entirely creditable. Byron has put on record his own high opinion of Ariosto in the following lines:

> The first will make an epoch with his lyre
> And fill the earth with feats of chivalry;
> His fancy like a rainbow, and his fire
> Like that of heaven immortal, and his thought
> Borne onward with a wing that cannot tire.
> Pleasure shall like a butterfly new caught
> Flutter her lovely pinions o'er his theme,
> And art itself seem into nature wrought
> By the transparency of his bright dream.
>
> *The Prophecy of Dante*, III, 110–119.

As might be expected, Shelley did not care for the *Orlando Furioso*, but if Keats' circumstances had been different he might well have shown himself a more appreciative and understanding lover of the poem than any of his contemporaries; for the intense and accurate vision of such pieces as *The Eve of S. Mark* or *The Eve of S. Agnes* is akin to the best in Ariosto.

It is not, however, only among the poets that we can find admirers of the *Orlando Furioso* at this time. Lord Metcalfe, when a boy at Eton, kept a diary in which he, on several occasions, records that he read Ariosto with Shaw, Nevill and other friends. Lord Holland inherited his uncle's taste for the poem, and doubtless Macaulay was not the sole untitled member of the Whig circle who could have proved his allegiance by a knowledge of Ariosto. Panizzi's edition of Boiardo and Ariosto, Stewart Rose's painstaking translation of the *Furioso*, and several other partial editions and translations, are evidence that during the first thirty or five and thirty years of the nineteenth century the *Orlando Furioso* was not losing its place in the public favour. Then, rather suddenly, there comes a change. Browning and Tennyson were both lovers of things Italian but neither of them appears to have felt any interest in Ariosto, and it is certain that he was not one of their favourites. The standard *Life of Tennyson* contains several of his criticisms on native and foreign bards, but not a single reference to Ariosto, and, speaking at a venture, it may be said that it would probably be difficult to find a single prominent and representative Victorian who had any affection for, or even much knowledge of, the *Orlando Furioso*. D. G. Rossetti, in spite of his Italian blood, only cared for it in his youth. His sonnet on the *Ruggiero and Angelica* of Ingres is inaccurate in at least one particular, and, what is much more important, little in harmony with the spirit of the original poem.

It may be that this change of taste was connected with the growing interest of England in Germany and German literature. Never before or since have the ideals of the two countries been so nearly alike as during the reign of Frederick William IV. A knowledge of German thought and scholarship was becoming indispensable to the learned, and German was tending to take the place of Italian as the second foreign language of the educated Englishman. Mrs Elton could air her scraps of Italian and Anne Elliot show a competent acquaintance with that tongue, but heroines born fifty years later would scarce have been similarly accomplished. However that may be, the interest felt in the *Orlando Furioso* waned rapidly after 1830 and has never revived. Among the few attempts to revive it the latest, that of Professor Nicholson, might have been attended with more success if he had not published his *Genius of Ariosto* at a peculiarly unfortunate moment.

F I N I S

Index

For EU product safety concerns, contact us at Calle de José Abascal, 56–1°, 28003 Madrid, Spain or eugpsr@cambridge.org.

www.ingramcontent.com/pod-product-compliance
Ingram Content Group UK Ltd.
Pitfield, Milton Keynes, MK11 3LW, UK
UKHW020315140625
459647UK00018B/1890